Two's Up

Memoirs of a Borstal boy

By

Kris Gray

Published by

FIVE MINUTE FICTION PUBLISHING
Calne
Wiltshire
SN11 9EB

www.five-minute-fiction.com
www.twos-up.com

First published in Great Britain 2010

First edition

Copyright © Kris Gray 2010

Kris Gray has asserted his right under the Copyright, Designs and Patents
Act 1988 to be identified as the author of this work

ISBN 9780956776204

Printed in Germany by
Verlag Lindemann
Stiftstrasse 49
63075 Offenbach

Cover design by Babz Bell www.photobabe.co.uk

This book is dedicated to my wonderful wife Ziggy who encouraged me to write this and put up with me locking myself away in the office for hours on end to do it. Also to the lad's who were there with me at the time, if you recognise yourself here I hope I've done you justice. Finally to Moira who had twos up on the entire period.

The Prologue

In the summer of 1970 I was living in Earls Court in two rooms with two other guys, I was seventeen and had only left school the year before. I'd already experimented with most pharmaceuticals including cannabis, cocaine, assorted barbiturates, uppers, downers and most importantly LSD. Heroin on the other hand had always been a no, no, mainly due to my fear of needles, no way could I stick one in my veins!

I first moved there, to join a band but that's another story, I had been working as a teleprinter operator with the then GPO. It didn't take long for me to tire of that occupation because as a teenager I was well underpaid; I soon realised that the guys I was scoring my drugs from were doing quite nicely thank you. So I decided I would go into the cannabis supply business. At first I would buy an ounce of cannabis for ten pounds, really ten pounds, and cut it up into fifteen pound deals and sell them on.

This led me to progress to buying a weight at a time, sixteen ounces, one pound. In those days that amount would cost around £90-£120 and could return a profit of at least double.

During the summer of 1970 I was doing well, earning in excess of two hundred pounds a week, a shed load of money in those days. That's when I met Moira, she's another story, but, in a way integral to this one. For those heady three months of June till September we were living the high life until one of my trusted suppliers ripped me off. He was supposed to bring me two weights, for which I had already given him the cash, however he decided a holiday in the West Indies was a better idea, never trust a drugs dealer.

That hit me hard, not just in my pocket but there were not many people you could get that kind of quantity from in those days and to be honest I was still a bit green. If that hadn't been enough to set me on a different path the next incident should have shown me the writing on the wall in bloody great big capital letters.

In desperation I went out one night to Brixton to score, in those days a white man alone was asking for trouble but I naively thought as I saw them as brothers they would see me the same way. So armed with my last £60 I set off to try and get myself something to sell.

To cut a long story short, especially as this is only the prologue, I had a fruitless night and came back safely, but empty handed, this turned out to be a blessing in disguise.

At the time Moira and I were living on the West Cromwell Road about 25 yards from the junction with Warwick Road. That evening as I returned, somewhat dejected, from the Warwick Road entrance of the Earls Court Road tube station I saw two men standing at the entrance of the house where my flat was. People come and go all time but these two guys had an aura of Fuzz about them so I hung back.

Within a few moments they went inside, I just knew that they were police and looking for me, what should I do? I knew they were looking for me and wouldn't give up. I had no drugs but I did have sixty quid that would take some explaining. I found a call box and dialled the flat number, one of our flat mates, Jenny answered and I asked for Moira. With a couple of questions I managed to ascertain that I had been correct and the police were in fact in the flat waiting for me. I told her I would be there in a few minutes and not to worry.

I secreted the sixty notes inside my underpants, surmising they wouldn't go so far as a strip search, believing that they had caught me by surprise.

Then I walked into the lion's den.

This is where I met DS Jones (real name) for the first time; I gave a good impression of surprise. DS Jones told me that he had information that there were stolen goods on the premises and proceeded to search. There was a paper bag with some minute particles of cannabis inside that he looked in but ignored, I should have seen the light then but I didn't.

After a casual search of my pockets, without finding the sixty notes, they left. I knew my card had been marked and I had to move on. Some friends had moved into a new house in Clapham Junction with a spare room so Moira and I chose to move in with them. However I decided to make a last sting to ease our way having been presented with a perfect opportunity when a couple of guys came to score half a weight.

I agreed to get this for them and we met at the flat in West Cromwell Road where they handed over the sixty pounds that I absconded with and moved to Clapham. The money lasted for a few weeks until I decided I needed to get back into the cannabis supply business.

However I was then short of cash to score.

Moira and I had, during this time, had met up with a guy by the name of Cliff. He was, like us, at a bit of a loose end and I managed to talk him into taking my chequebook and cashing it all. He went from bank to bank cashing cheques for thirty pounds a time which gave us over six hundred pounds. I had to report my chequebook and cash card as being stolen in Oxford Street, which I did, and everything appeared to go according to plan.

The plan was to buy a half weight and get back into cannabis dealing, sadly that backfired. Unbeknown to me Cliff also had a stolen Barclaycard, at the time a new item that, on the surface was easy to scam. Cliff's card was on the stolen list and when he was trying to draw some cash from a bank he was pounced on and arrested.

Unfortunately for me he still had my chequebook and cheque card on him and guess who picked up on the connection? You've got it DS Jones.

DS Jones turned up on my doorstep in Clapham, he found the cash in no time and with a line that I fell for, that a cashier would recognise her writing, I gave up that I had been involved with Cliff and was dragged off to face the music at Kensington Police station.

It turned out that the two guys I ripped off had been sent to set me up by DS Jones. He was understandably pissed off when I didn't arrive with the drugs so that he could bust me but got his revenge with the cheques.

My parents bailed me out but on the condition that Moira and I went to live with them until the case came up. This we did, having a somewhat strained Christmas and New Year 1970/71 until my case came up on the 25th of January 1971. My lawyer wasn't too optimistic about my chances of a light sentence and he was right.

Cliff, who was over twenty-one, was sentenced to six months in jail and I was sentenced to a term in Borstal, which I very soon found out meant a minimum of six months to a maximum of two years.

I made it my mission to get out as close to six months as I possibly could.

Here is my story, all of which is true, there was a Borstal named Gaynes Hall in Huntingdonshire and all these people really existed, however other than my name, I have changed the others to protect the guilty.

+++++++++++++

Chapter One
I Didn't Mean To Do It Your Honour, Honestly

Where do I start? At the end I think is the best place as it is almost the same place as where it all started, I'm sitting in the library at Gaynes Hall just as I had done some seven months before, when I arrived.

Only this time I was going home.

This time the sun was shining as I waited with my fellow dischargees for the bus that would take us to the station and freedom. Freedom that those few months before had seemed like a lifetime away, trust me those months went very slowly.

Still, that first day had seemed like paradise after The Scrubs, for uninformed 'The Scrubs' as it is well known, is Wormwood Scrubs prison. It was built between 1875 and 1891 by convict labour and in the early seventies acted, partly, as an allocation centre. This meant that convicted felons were taken there to be assessed, then, sent to a suitable prison to serve out their sentences, including Borstal Boys.

I will never forget my first night there as I arrived in a bus, with a number of other felons, from the Inner London Quarter Sessions at the Elephant and Castle. I had been waiting for, what seemed like forever, in the cells at the court after being sentenced by the sombre judge for my heinous crimes. Cliff, my partner in crime, and I had been one of the first cases of the day; being over twenty-one he received a six-month jail sentence so he would probably be out in four. I, on the other hand, had at least six months to look forward to, even as much as two years, it didn't seem fair at the time.

My parents and Moira had been at the court with me, mother had pinned my long hair up so it looked as if it was short, she thought it might make a difference, it didn't. When the beak spoke the magic words 'Take him down' Moira burst into tears and that was the last I saw of her for a week as my father was comforting her.

My lawyer was allowed to come and visit me in the cell but no one else. I naively asked if an appeal was likely to be successful. He replied that I could only appeal against the sentence, as I was clearly guilty. However, it was unlikely to succeed and may only cause me more stress, better to knuckle down and get on with it. He also thought that it would be most unlikely for me to serve two years that helped to feel slightly better.

So with nothing else to do but reflect on my stupidity for what seemed like a week, I did just that curled up on wooden bed in the corner of the cell.

Eventually they came to take me away; I was led up to the exit where I was handcuffed to another guy then taken on to a bus. My fellow passenger didn't speak a word throughout the entire journey, which seemed never ending, from South London to The Scrubs in West London. I was grateful for his silence; I had nothing to say to him anyway, I was scared shitless, images of Brendan Behan's famous book came to mind and made me feel sick at the thought.

Cliff was closer to the back handcuffed to someone else, I was glad; I didn't really want to speak to him either, plus, I was pretty sure he would have nothing good to say to me, as it was, mostly, my fault he was there.

We arrived at the 'pearly gates' in darkness, I don't know what time it was as my watch, along with everything else I had on me except my cigarettes, had been taken and put away until my release. It was the end of January and the darkness gave me a false sense of time but I guessed it to be around five. I looked out of the window at the floodlit walls as we passed through the gate.

I wasn't really struck by what lay ahead of me until we were led into the reception area. There was a queue to see the reception officer who was a crew cropped, fat bellied screw who took great sadistic pleasure in confiscating my cigarettes and offering them round to the established inmates.

'Name?'

'Gray, Kristopher Edwin'

'Date of birth?'

'29th of September 1952'

'Religion?'

'I have no religion.' His eyes that hadn't moved from the form slowly came up to meet mine.

'W'dya mean no poxy religion? You must've been baptised into somfing!'

'Why?' I asked with a naive braveness

'Don't be cheeky with me you little atheist bastard or I'll come down on you like a ton of bricks.' A predictable cliché 'All right, no religion.' I had temporarily won the day. 'Now move on!'

I left by another door at the end of the room, which led me to an old lag (long term prisoner) standing by a table full of plates that were covered in what I guessed to be food of some kind.

'Take a plate and a mug of tea and go in there' I did as I was told and followed his finger. Inside were some tables and chairs and a toilet, not exactly home but it would have to do for the time being. I played with what looked like baked beans for a while, trying to pluck up the courage to try them. The mug of tea looked as though it's previous residence had been the china bowl in the corner of the room. I took a sip, no sugar, which in those days I still used in tea. What else did I expect? Still, it was wet and my mouth was so dry I would have drunk just about anything.

For a while I sat reading the age-old graffiti along the walls until Cliff came into the room. We looked at each other for a moment then he sat down away from me, I wasn't surprised. Some of the writings were dated, 1947? Christ, hadn't they painted the place since then? As I was half way through the tea a smaller lad, possibly younger than I was, came and sat next to me.

'Alo mate, I'm fucking starving!' how could he be? I felt as if I'd never eat again and he was shovelling the muck into his mouth as if it was his last meal 'what's the matter, don't you want yours?' he asked eyeing the mess on my plate, I shook my head. 'Great!' he yelled as he scrapped everything from my plate onto his.

I sat watching him with dismay; he seemed completely unaffected by the whole experience.

'Been inside before?' I asked

'Yeah, did three months proovie last year.' I must have looked puzzled 'Approved school, ha! Real laugh it was too!'

Hysterical!

'What about you?'

'Never.'

'You'll get used to it, down for Borstal are ya?' I nodded my head 'Yeah the old six t' two, you'll probably be out by this time next year.' I wanted to believe him, I was expecting to be shut way for close to the two years 'What you in for?'

'Ripped off my bank account, you?'

'Hi-jacking' one of the big time, I was later to discover that his hi-jacking went to the extent of stealing a mini-van. 'I'll probably get an open place, you might as well, do drugs do ya?'

'Some.'

'Junkie are ya?'

'No just smoke a bit of shit'

'Eh?'

'Cannabis.' Just as I said the magic word a big black guy came through the door, eyes wide with expectation as he sidled up beside me.

'You got any maan?' whispered in my ear with a thick Jamaican accent

'Wish I had.' I mumbled back

'Ras-claat! Jeez man I wish I had a spliff right now, I could do my bird standing on my head! How'z me gonna get troo the next cupla years widout a spliff?'

'Guess you'll have to stay upright then.' I quipped

'Wot you 'ere for?' my pirate friend asked him

'GBH, greevus bodily 'arm' obviously the peaceful qualities of the weed had eluded him.

Gradually the room began to fill with jabbering new arrivals from various other courts of the capital, telling way out yarns as to why and how they had come to be there, amazing how many of them were innocent! I found it difficult to speak to anybody, everything seemed so surreal and I was waiting for someone to come and tell me it was all a big mistake.

Eventually we were told to file back into the corridor where we were to wait for the doctor. Nobody stayed with him for more than a couple of minutes, I could hear the procedure with the guy who went in front of me.

'Anything wrong with you?'

'Well my foot.......'

'Good nothing, had any serious illnesses?'

'No but my foot......'

9

'Drugs, are you on any drugs, heroin or cocaine?'

'No but my foot really hu....'

'Get out!.....Next!'

'But what about my foot?'

'You'll have two broken legs if you don't get out of here now! Next!' that was me.

'Anything wrong with you?'

'No.' he looked at me with a narrowed eye, I thought I had to leave so turned to go.

'Where do you think you're going? I haven't finished with you yet, any serious illnesses?'

'I've had TB of the lungs.' He grunted and made a note on the file.

'Drugs, are you on any drugs, heroin or cocaine?'

'No.'

'Are you sure, you look like a druggie to me?'

'Positive.'

'Look I don't want you going cold turkey on me in the middle of the night.' His eyes narrowed even further.

'Really, no drugs.' I emphasised the point.

'Right, get out.........Next!'

As I emerged from the room I was immediately directed to another where they would take my fingerprints, again. Surely they had enough copies of them to open an exhibition at the Royal Academy? The screw performing this torture was young and the first I'd seen with any kind of faint smile on his face. He must have been new, I suspect smiling was difficult for anyone working in such a dump as Wormwood Scrubs.

He stopped for a brief moment to give me a strange look then put his hand to my head.

'What's this then?' and proceeded to remove one of mother's hair pins 'Hoping to pick the lock were we?'

'No just....' He then removed all the pins to let my shoulder length hair drop down so that he could flick it with his fingers and started to laugh.

'What, did you think it would make you look innocent if you had short hair? Seems such a pity, they'll have all that off tomorrow, must have taken a while to grow it?'

'It'll grow again, still might get away with it' he started to laugh.

'You're not going to try that old religion chestnut are you, going to be a Sheik?' It had crossed my mind but I'd nixed that one with the 'no religion' bit. 'You'll be close to bald mate!'

'Maybe I can just hide it under my hat,' that amused him as well, he'd finished by now and pointed me in the direction of the stores where I could trade in my clothes for something new with designer arrows all over it. There were two older men handing out the latest fashions.

'How's life?' I asked one of them

'Much the same after twenty odd years, how's yours looking Sonny Jim?' I later found out he was a lifer and one of the longest serving cons in the place. 'Now let's see how badly we can stitch you up on your clothing, waist size?'

'Thirty two.' Those were the days!

'Here's a pair of thirty six, shoes?' handing me a pair without my answering. 'These are size nine, they ok for you?' I didn't answer, I didn't want to give him the satisfaction of knowing they were a size too big. 'Here are two shirts, don't wear the second one or we'll have to wash them both when you move on'

'In that case I'll make sure I do.'

'Just you dare.'

'I may even wipe my arse with it.' He threw a bag at me that was filled with my survival kit for the duration. Everything I would need, two sheets, one blanket, a bed cover, a pillow case, two plastic plates, plastic cutlery, a mug, a razor without a blade, toothbrush, no paste and a bar of soap less soap.

'Don't loose anything or you'll have to pay for it, here's your best bib and tucker' he tossed a blue jacket and a pair of grey trousers at me 'Don't worry if they don't fit, you probably won't need to wear them anyway.'

'OK sunshine' the older one chipped in again, 'let's have you stripped off so we can see what you've got.'

They gave me a set of underwear that would have fit Billy Bunter. My suit was bundled into a box with my name on it and placed on a shelf along with God knows how many more. I was then directed to another room with baths in it. The water ran fast, at least it was hot and I was able to waste a little time there. It was really quite an impersonal room. The wall between the next one and mine was only about five feet high and the door came right out of a western movie.

'Come on Jesus,' a screw rattled the door 'we've got a cosy little peter (cell) waiting for you tonight so get moving.' The face of my fat friend from the reception appeared and disappeared quickly, much to my relief. I dried and dressed as quickly as I could to rejoin the others who were waiting for me. Borstal boys were taken one way whilst others were taken another. I looked towards Cliff who nodded at me and that was the last time I ever saw him.

We were led out of the reception area in our new clothes; it wasn't easy walking in oversized trousers and shoes. The shirt I was wearing had half a sleeve missing which made it a little draughty; I made a note to change it for the spare when I could. It was raining as we passed barred windows and tall cellblocks; just like another world inside a world. It seemed as if nothing else existed beyond the high walls that were heavily floodlit and garnished with barbed wire.

As I stepped into the Borstal wing I could feel the bad, even evil vibes ringing out from every corner of the building. I looked up to see that there were four levels including the ground floor with wire meshing, to stop would be suicides, between them.

'Right!' barked the leading screw 'Harper, Smith and Davies in 'ere, look sharpish lads, lights out soon.' The cell allocation had begun 'Next! Swanson, Merrick and Bates in 'ere, swiftly lads I 'aven't got all night.' Three more were herded into the next cell. 'Next! Clifford, Jones and Gray into your little 'ome from 'ome!'

The three of us found ourselves inside the smallest space you can imagine. It had originally been built in the last century for one person and not three. As the door banged savagely behind me I went right off the top of my head. This was really happening to me and it was just like a bad trip. I was almost hallucinating just as if I were on an LSD trip, I wanted out right there and then. My brain was screaming out loud that I would never do it again so please could I go home.

No one was listening.

No one cared.

Little Big Time the highjacker and Ras-claat were yapping away constantly about their criminal achievements and how they'd been caught. Funny how it was always somebody else's fault.

I couldn't talk at all; I was just too spaced out of my mind to think of anything else but getting out. I was still trying to convince myself that it was all a big mistake and that someone would soon come and set me free.

But they never did.

Ras-claat jumped up to the top bunk while I took the one below. Big mistake, the mattress was in five pieces, the last of which was missing. I made up the bed as best I could and lay on it fully clothed, it was not warm, in fact it was positively freezing.

The cell door opened again.

'Here's a letter each for you and a pen to share, I'll be back for it, when you've finished pop it in the post box by the office. I don't know when it will get delivered what with the post office strike but it'll give you something to do.'

On January 20th 1971, five days before, the Post Office Workers Union went on strike for seven weeks, during this time it was impossible for me to write home but due to private delivery services Moira and my parents could write to me. It was a very long painful period, bad enough being locked up but having so little contact with the outside world was really hard.

The lights went out dead on ten. I just lay staring into space for most of the night, only catching a few moments sleep here and there. It was so noisy, people shouting out the windows all night long threatening each other and banging on the heating pipe that ran right through the cell block from one end to another. This would continue, almost as a ritual, every night that I was there. What was wrong with these people? Didn't they need to sleep? I suppose caged animals behave like this and I guess that was what we were, caged animals.

I suppose I eventually got some sleep but I'm pretty sure it wasn't a great deal!

+++++++++++++++++

I was awake long before the key rattled in the lock and the heavy door flew open.

'Slop out!' this meant one had to empty the unpleasant contents, if any, of one's bedpan. The door had been opened for the three of us to do just that. The main toilets were dark and ancient with a large porcelain bowl in the corner where everybody emptied their pans. It was revolting. We also had a container each enabling us to take fresh, cold, water back to our cell for washing and cleaning it out.

14

I hurried back as quickly as I could, I didn't like being outside with anyone else, and I just wanted to be alone.

Soon we were summoned to breakfast, I didn't move, food was the last thing on my mind, especially as I had a good idea what it would be like.

'Don't you want any grub mate?' asked Little Big Time, I just shook my head. 'Can I have it then?' I nodded and followed him to the breakfast queue where I collected a plate of, guess what, porridge, an egg and two slices of bread with a pat of margarine. I kept the bread and handed the rest to LBT, I didn't really want it but I forced some down with the truly terrible tea.

Later some cons came round with a trolley to collect the empty trays leaving me to continue contemplating my position on my jigsaw puzzle of a bed, and it wasn't looking good.

Before very long before the door opened again and another screw came in brandishing a clipboard.

'You three wait outside, you're all due to see the social worker. After that move up to the second level to a new cell, listen carefully, Clifford 2/89, Jones 2/25, and Gray 2/64. Leave your kits here and come back to collect them after you've been to see the Wing Governor.'

He led us across the cellblock to some seats outside another cell being used as an office; I just sat there, not saying a word to anyone. Ras-claat went in first, the door stayed open but I wasn't able to hear what was said, I didn't really want to anyway.

He was in there for about ten to fifteen minutes before he came back to sit next to me.

'Gray!' I made my way sheepishly inside where a middle aged woman sat with a smile on her face, I wondered what it was she had to smile about. Going home that night perhaps?

'Sit down young man, Kristopher is it?'

'I prefer Kris'

'OK Kris, now whilst you are here you'll be seeing a few different people and taking some tests to find out more about you. We need to know the best Borstal to send you to; they are all very different you know. Now I see you obtained cash and goods by deception, was it to buy drugs?' her eyes had shifted to my, still, shoulder length hair.

'No.' it was true as far as her meaning of the question was.

'Good, do you use drugs?'

'No.' I lied

'Good, now were you working at the time of your arrest?'

'Yes'

'And what was it you were doing?'

'I'm a musician.' Her eyes narrowed.

'Are you sure you're not on drugs then?'

'To be honest I have smoked cannabis but I've no interest in anything else.' She looked unconvinced but let it slide, what was this bloody obsession with drugs anyway?

'Good, so what do you intend to do once you are released?'

'I would like to go back to it.'

'Back to what?' trying to trip me up.

'Back to being a musician.' I replied

'Don't you think something else would be better, something a bit steadier?'

'You mean like a proper job?'

'Yes I suppose that is what I mean?'

'You sound like my mother.' I laughed, it also brought a smile to her face 'I know I can make a good living, I'm quite good you know.'

'I see,' she didn't really 'will you continue to smoke cannabis as well?'

'I don't think that would be a very good idea, do you?' I'm sure I detected a brief smile at that remark.

'Do you have a girlfriend on the outside?'

'Yes I do, we were living together before I came here.'

'Do you think she will wait for you?'

'I hope so.'

'So do I young man, does she take drugs?' there she went with the drugs issue again.

'No!' I was getting quite indignant now. Her eyes narrowed, maybe I had overstepped the mark and she was getting the wrong impression of me, but then the frown melted and the smile returned.

'OK, well that is all from me, go back and wait outside whilst I speak to Mr Jones and then you will go to see the wing governor.'

I mumbled a thank you, stood up and left the room to sit back outside whilst LBT took my place in the office. I had only been there a few moments when a big beefy screw grabbed me by the arm and lifted me from the seat.

'You've a date with the barber son, this way' and proceeded to drag me along to another cell where the barber was performing, despite my protestations that I was due to see the wing governor. 'It won't take long and he'll still be there when it's all over!'

There was a long queue, great, I thought, I'll disappear when this monkey has gone but oh no, he took me right down to the front. Someone was already in the chair, half shorn, but he was removed so that I could have priority treatment.

'Make it as short as you can.' Was the instruction he gave to the barber?

'With the greatest of pleasure.' Suddenly there was an audience of prison officers hanging around the door to watch and laugh as I was shorn almost bald. Deep down inside I was hurting really bad; I'd never been so humiliated in my life. However, I just laughed along with them saying it would grow again.

'Not for the next two years it won't chum.' That was a smack in the face, two years? Was I really going to spend two years in a place like this? 'Right back to the wing governor for you.' The smirking bastard said as he hauled me out of the chair and marched me over to his office where the wing governor was waiting. 'Gray sir.'

'Where has he been, I called for him ten minutes ago?'

'Barber sir, hair was halfway down his back.' Bit of an exaggeration but I wasn't going to argue.

'All right.' He motioned for him to leave. The haircut had freaked me out and just about finished me off; my head was definitely not where it should have been to be able to deal with another interrogation. The governor turned his attention back to me and his voice brought me some of the way back to earth. 'Do you drink?'

'I'm sorry?'

'I want to know if you drink alcohol.'

'I like a pint or two.' I was stuttering a bit but managed to bring it into check 'Not much really.'

'Just as well, you wont miss not having any here, do you smoke?'

'Not much.'

'Drugs?'

'Only cannabis,' couldn't say much else as I had already confessed this to the social worker.

'What about heroin, you look a little pale?'

'Never!' I was most emphatic.

'Roll your sleeves up,' I immediately obeyed. He grunted when there were no track marks to be found on my needle free veins. 'All right, all right put your sleeves back.' He looked back to his paperwork. 'What do you intend to do on your release?'

Not again? How could they imagine I could think of such things when release seemed light years away?

'I, I'm feeling a little bit detached and scared at the moment,' and I was, scared shitless in fact, not knowing what lay ahead of me. For the first time since coming into his office I saw him smile, apparently he hadn't lost the ability to do so.

'You'll soon get over the initial shock and settle down to do your time.' I sincerely wished that I had his confidence.

'How long do you think I'll serve?' I asked him.

'It's hard to say, it all depends on you, where you're sent, how you adapt and how you behave but I don't suppose you'll do much more than a year.'

A year! That was a lifetime to me but better than the two I was expecting. I left his office with a newfound hope, then taken back to my cell to collect my kit and make my way to cell 2/64.

++++++++++++++++++++

The door to cell 2/64 was locked so I had to wait, kit in arms, to be let in; I looked through the peephole to see one other person inside.

In a short space of time a screw came to let me in, the other lad inside beamed a smile and leapt up to help me. I was only just through the door when it slammed shut behind me

'Company at last, come on let's get you settled in,' he said in a thick Brummie accent. There was another bed on its side up against the wall, which he put down to help me set out my bedding. 'You're not allowed to make up your bed until after eight, so, just put your cover on and fold up your bedding for now.' I was a bit wary of him, was he a friend or a foe?

'I'm Bob,' I swung my kit onto the bed as my new cellmate held out his hand with a genuine smile on his face.

'I'm Kris,' I replied as I took his hand with a grip as firm as his, I do so hate people who shake with the proverbial 'wet fish'.

'Welcome, well, sort of,' we both laughed, feeling somewhat naked after my visit to the barber I stroked the stubble on the back of my neck. 'They just lopped off all my hair,' I managed a half smile, 'Christ it's cold in here.'

'Yeah, sorry and it gets worst at night, as you can see there's virtually no glass in those windows up there and the wind just howls through 'em. I should be getting my Borstal allocation in a few days so I should be shipping out soon, to somewhere a bit warmer with a bit of luck.' Luck? Yes I suppose from that point of view it would be. 'When did you come in, last night?'

'Yes,'

'Got any burn?' (Tobacco)

'No all I had was confiscated when I came in and shared around the reception officers.'

'Typical, so I guess you could do with a smoke.'

'You bet, I haven't had a fag since before I was sent down, I could have smoked a hundred last night.'

'Well you can share mine for as long as it lasts, you'll get paid on Friday, one and ten pence, that will buy you a quarter of an ounce, a packet of papers and a box of matches, here.' He gave me a roll up made from that wonderful smoking mixture, Black Shag, probably the most revolting smoke known to man but more than welcome in the circumstances. 'Keep your defts (dog ends) for when we run out, we can re-roll them to make a few more.'

The thought of re-rolled black shag made me shudder but no doubt I'd smoke them when the time came.

We lay back on our bed in silence for a few moments, savouring the nicotine as it surged through our blood vessels. The tobacco was really strong and was making me feel a little light headed. It didn't stop me sucking it in though.

'Do you have a pen Bob? I could use it to write my letter home.'

'Sure, er I wonder,' he passed the pen over and gave me a sheepish look 'er could you do something for me when you've finished?' I was warming very quickly to this refugee from Birmingham.

'If I can, of course, what?' he hesitated for a few moments.

'I can't read or write, would you write to my parents for me if I tell you what to say?' Poor bastard I thought locked up a long way from home and unable to write to his nearest and dearest. I wrote his letter first, he was from Coventry so there wasn't much chance of a visit from them whilst he was in the Scrubs.

+++++++++++++++

After a better night's sleep than I'd had the night before, well marginally, the slop out hour came once more. The toilet and shower area at the end of the cellblock was an impersonal place. You couldn't have a shit or a bath in private, the doors were half size so that the screws, or anyone come to that, could look over to watch you. Lucky for me I hadn't eaten in two days so the urge for a number two wasn't there.

Today was time to see the Vocational Guidance Officer who insisted on asking me the same old questions, the answers to which he didn't like either. He had an idea that I would be well advised to take up one of the courses that would be available to me in engineering or something similar.

It was a short interview but I had to wait around for what seemed like forever, with the other new arrivals that I came in with, to be taken back to our block. It was lunchtime, something I still couldn't get excited about, but as I stepped back into the cellblock a screw pulled me to one side.

'Gray?' I acknowledged the friendly call 'You have visitors, step this way.' It could only have been my parents; this would make my day, so I followed him across what seemed like miles of prison courtyard to the visiting rooms.

I was led into a small room where everything I had on me, which was, one dog end and a scrap of paper, were removed and put into a numbered bag. I was then searched from head to toe before being sat behind a small table. There were only three others in the room waiting for visitors.

When my parents came in with Moira as well I could feel the tears welling up in my eyes. They didn't recognise me immediately as I saw them scan the other faces in the room. They hadn't seen me without my long hair for quite some time.

Suddenly I just broke down and really cried. I could see my mother was trying to hold back the tears but father managed a forced smile.

Moira was crying too.

'Happy birthday!' I tried to laugh through the tears, unsuccessfully, she tried to laugh as well, it was indeed, her birthday.

'How is it?' my father asked

'About as awful as you'd expect,' I choked as I spoke 'the cell is freezing, the food's poison, the treatment varies but could be worse and the boredom is likely to drive me mad. I've been given three books to read and finished one already having spent about ninety percent of the time banged up.'

'On your own?' Dad asked

'No, I'm sharing with a nice enough lad who is keeping me supplied with the worst kind of tobacco you can imagine. We talk and smoke, smoke and talk, smoke and think, have long silences but otherwise we have a great time.' I didn't mean to sound bitter but I was.

I told them of the people I had spoken to since my arrival, they listened attentively as I talked and chain-smoked mother's cigarettes. She offered me a packet to take in with me but I knew they wouldn't let me keep it so I declined.

'I should be out within a year, maybe even Christmas'

'Really!' All their faces lit up, they, like me had obviously been expecting the worst, two full years 'Oh I hope so,' mother continued, that would be all the Christmas present I'd need.'

'Will you come back to me when you get out?' Moira asked

'Will you wait for me?'

'Of course I will.' It was a wonderful surprise to see them all, especially on Moira's birthday.

Prison regulations and warders being what they are when they say visits last half an hour, on the dot of thirty minutes all visitors are herded out. They all gave me a quick hug before leaving, unusual for my father to show such affection.

'Keep your chin up mate,' he said as they headed for the door, 'we'll be back next month.'

Then those left behind are shaken down once more in case we try to smuggle in any contraband. My dog end and scrap of paper were returned to me before I was led back to my punishment. I now felt worse than I had before they came; somehow seeing them brought home the reality of it all once again.

+++++++++++++++

I never ate a full meal during my time in Wormwood Scrubs, just couldn't face it, let alone swallow it. I would have the suppertime cake with a mug of tea but very little other than that. Bob would go for his meals; he seemed to have adjusted to the bilge they served without much trouble. Sometimes I would get mine so that he could have that as well. So with the lack of input I only had to make an output a couple of times during the ten days I was there. I just couldn't do it in the cell in front of Bob, not to mention how impolite it would have been to add the smell to what else was in there. Holding your balance at the same time would have been next to impossible anyway.

On the third night in the cell with Bob I suddenly had a brain wave.

'Battleships!' I cried

'Beg pardon?' Bob replied

'Battleships,' I repeated, 'we could play battleships.' I could see that Bob had absolutely no idea what I was talking about so I set about explaining the rudiments of the game. He was most enthusiastic about the idea after I went over it a couple of times. Paper, however, was the problem; we didn't have any until Bob hit on an idea. Between us we had six library books that had over thirty blank pages in them, so we tore out two and started to play.

'A6,' my shot first.

'Splash, C8.'

'Splash, B9.'

'Splash, E5.'

'Bang!' Got me.

And so we played until lights out, stopping for a few brief moments to have a piss or roll another cigarette from Bob's rapidly depleting supply of Black Shag. Payday had come and gone but it would appear that neither of us would see it until we had been moved to our respective Borstal.

+++++++++++++++

The only excitement on the following day was Bob's news that he had been allocated to a Borstal and he wasn't pleased.

'Wales! Fucking Usk in Wales man,' he began to mimic the Wing Governor, 'we try to send boys to a Borstal near their home but we felt Usk was the best place for you.' Best suited for me my arse, how the fuck do they think my folks are going to get to fucking Wales to see me. I'll never get a visit from them, they don't have a car and.....'

24

I could see that he wanted to cry but was forcing the tears back because of me, I wanted to look the other way for him to be able to let it all out but I didn't.

He should have cried.

I wondered where I would be sent. There was a big map on the ground floor wall by the office where all the Borstals were marked. I'd heard stories about a great many of them, probably vastly exaggerated but frightening never the less. Usk didn't sound so bad but the worst was, without a doubt, Portland on the south coast. It was a closed Borstal, a bit like an adult prison, where the worst offenders, especially those with violent crimes, were sent. All the tough cases, I shuddered at the thought but was fairly confident that I wouldn't go.

Rumour had it that there was at least one razoring, i.e. attacks with a razor, usually on the face, every week. I also heard that all the new arrivals were given a welcome beating, to see how tough they were. Bob was pretty sure I wasn't the type to be sent there, fingers crossed. I did meet a strange lad who worked in the kitchens; he told me that he was asking to be sent there. He didn't seem the type who would fit into what I'd been told about the place. For his sake I hoped that he wouldn't get his way.

Some Borstals were known as 'open' because there were no cells but dormitories and even they had no locks on them. I prayed that I would get one of those. The name that kept cropping up as the elite institution was Gaynes Hall.

+++++++++++++++++

I spent the entire morning of the next day in a classroom with a whole bunch of guys including LBT and Ras-claat. We spent all the time doing elementary puzzles like putting shapes together and solving simple word games that were designed to see how cleaver we were, or weren't as the case may be.

When I arrived back at the cell Bob had gone, it was customary that when you were allocated to a Borstal you were moved up to a cell on the third floor. Up there Bob would wait for anything up to two months for the next available place on a transport to Usk. I knew it would be about another three days before I was allocated and unless I had a new cellmate it was going to be very lonely.

No one came.

I had my two remaining library books to read anyway.

It was Thursday, I'd been in The Scrubs for a week, seven days, which it felt like seven months already, and I still didn't know how to cope with it all. It was so cold in the cell, even though I had moved my bed to where Bob's had been, bang up against the heating pipe, and, although I was fully clothed in bed I was still frozen. I just wanted to get out of this awful fucking prison to a Borstal and get all of this shit over and done with.

It was a bloody cold Thursday!

Since Bob had gone I had nothing to smoke, sure I had about forty dog ends but no papers to roll a new one and no match to light it with either. I was just lying there freezing and dying for a smoke when a voice came from the cell next door in a heavy Welsh accent.

'Hey you in sixty four, this is sixty three, have you got any burn?' There was a small gap all around the pipe as it passed through the wall allowing such conversations to take place without raising your voice.

'Just a few defts,' I replied.

'Want to swap some for a few papers and some matches?'

'Sure,'

'OK I'll give you five papers, two matches and a bit of strike for half your stock.'

'Done!' I threaded fifteen dog ends wrapped up in a piece of paper, in a few moments back came the agreed exchange. I got to work straight away rolling a smoke; I split one of the matches with the pin Bob left me so that I could get two strikes out of one. I later perfected this art to enable me to make four strikes from one match.

When I lit the cigarette I'd made from five of the dog ends. I nearly choked to death, it was horrible and strong, I took the first puff deep into my lungs and my head started to swim. It felt as if I'd taken a couple of tokes of grass, it didn't make me feel sick, just a little dizzy for a few moments.

I lay there thinking about what the Chief Warden had told us the day after we came in, he was telling us the rules and regulations.

'See that little pot in the corner?' He pointed at the chamber pot, 'it's for your use when the cell door is locked and I don't want you posting little parcels out of the window. You're allowed to have newspapers and magazines, sorry, no girlie stuff, if you want a wank you'll have to use you're imagination.'

I was still chuckling at the memory when the lights went out suddenly, ten o'clock and I was feeling far from sleeping. I stood up on my bed to look out of the window across to the next block. People were shouting all the time from our block to theirs. Then there was the banging on the pipes; someone who was bored would use his mug to make music on them.

'Get off the fucking pipes!' Would come the shouts.

'Go fuck yourself.' Would come the reply

'It's me in 2/32 come and stop me.'

'I'll get you tomorrow you mouthy cunt!'

'Hey I'm in 2/32 don't try stitching me up you piece of shit, if you're not big enough to own up yourself stop banging on the fucking pipes!'

'Shut up arsehole or I'll do you in as well!'

This banter would go on well into the night until sleep finally overtook the aggression. The screws would ignore it, there wasn't much they could do to stop it anyway and apart from being a serious nuisance nothing ever came of it, well not whilst I was there anyway.

There was little freedom in sleep either, when you finally managed to get some that is. Every hour a screw did the rounds and if you didn't show any signs of life they would rattle the bolt on the door until you did.

'I'm here!' they might shout as well, as if we didn't know

It was so cold at night I had to sleep with my shirt on despite the fact that it was against the rules, as was nearly everything else in the place. Although the January wind blew through the broken windows I eventually caught forty winks. It wouldn't be long however before that bolt would rattle for the last time that night. Bringing me out of any escaping dreams I was having, to return to the cold, harsh reality of my predicament, I was still in prison.

The morning ritual was the same every day, your feet had to be out of bed and on the floor before the screw came back to open the door to slop out. As well as disposing of the night's contents of your bedpan you had to collect a pail of water to wash and shave in. You were then required to scrub the floor of the cell with the remainder. We weren't allowed to keep razor blades so one of the lads would bring one round every morning. Everybody had his own personal blade that was collected after breakfast. I didn't understand the logic in that, if you wanted to do some damage with yours you could easily do so, even in such a short space of time.

Even after a week inside I still found it very difficult to eat anything, not that anything they served was particularly appetising. In the oncoming months I never really did form a particular liking for the porridge they served up. So I generally skipped breakfast and lunch, the only thing I looked forward to was the late night cake.

On this particular day, not long after the morning hubbub had died away the cell door flew open.

'All right the laddie, get yourself downstairs outside the Wing Governors office, now boy, move it!' I'd spent the past couple of days since Bob had left banged up for the best part of twenty three hours each day. It was a bit of a relief to get out of my little box if only for a half hour or so.

I threaded my way along the landing and down the iron steps to the ground floor. I still felt somewhat overawed by what was happening to me but no longer frightened of every person who passed me as I had been to start with. I learnt quite quickly that a great number of them were just as disorientated as myself.

I knew where I was going so planted myself on one of the chairs outside the cell that had been converted to serve as an office. I recognised most of the faces around me; they had been on most of the other excursions I'd been to, although I didn't know any of their names. There was someone I recognised from the kitchens; we were on kind of nodding terms.

'You here for allocation?' he asked

'Guess so,' I replied 'is that what you're here for?'

'Yeah, where you hoping to go?'

'I don't really know, haven't given it a lot of thought, but I certainly don't want to go to the island of dreams.'

'What Portland?'

'Yeah, no way, I'm the strong silent type, peace loving that's me, just want to do my bird in the quietest possible way.'

'You don't want to believe all those stories, they're all bullshit put about to scare the bejeezus out of first timers.'

'It works.'

'You'll not go there, mark my words, you'll go some place cushy.'

'I hope so, I'd rather go to Devil's Island than Portland.'

'Devils Island, never heard of that one.'

'It's a French prison on an....' I could see I'd lost him 'never mind.'

Suddenly I saw Bob out of the corner of my eye as he came towards me; it was good to see him again. He told me briefly that he was moving out in another two weeks to Wales and seemed a lot happier about it. I guessed that now it was settled he had learnt to accept it, I was hoping I wouldn't be sent too far. He now had a job; most lads would get some kind of work to do whilst they waited to be moved out to a Borstal. Bob was working in the toy factory, which was probably one of the best jobs in the place.

He didn't really have much time to stop and natter so he slipped me a couple of burns and went on his way.

I never saw him again.

'Gray!' my name cut through the air like a knife and made me jump as if I hadn't been expecting it to be coming. I stood and followed the sound of the voice into the tiny room to stand before the imposing figure of the Wing Governor who smiled up at me. 'Sit down lad,' he indicated the chair to me, then, smiled again.

'Thank you sir.' I just about managed to say.

'Well young man, we've finally finished all our deliberations on you and have decided you will be best suited to go to Gaynes Hall, how do you feel about that?'

'I, I er really don't know sir.'

'It's in Hertfordshire which isn't too far from your home, just a little way up the A1. You seem to be an intelligent lad and I think that you will benefit from spending some time there, learn something from your stay there and don't go astray again.'

He had to be joking.

'Thank you sir,' I stuttered, not really knowing what I was thanking him for, and then I stood up and left the room.

Back at the cell I had to wait to be let back in. Once inside I laid back on my bed thinking about going to Gaynes Hall, it sounded like an ok place. Still I would be moved up to the third floor soon, hopefully with someone else and a job to do instead of going mad alone in this cell twenty three hours a day.

I picked up one of the books I had to read, something about jungle warfare in WW2, and settled down for a long read. Once again I ignored the call for lunch, still wasn't that interested in food and hadn't as yet eaten a full meal since my arrival.

I continued to read until the cell door rattled once again, could it be some company?

Sadly not, it was just a screw standing in the doorway.

'Gray, get yourself down to the main wing gate, you're going to have your mug shots done.'

Once again I was grateful to leave the confine of my shabby cell on the second floor to go for a short walk. I didn't really care where, just so long as it was something different to do.

The same familiar faces were there, those who had followed me through all the other stages of allocation. Now all our pictures need to be taken to complete the files.

Just before we were led out of the block the lad from the kitchen, who I was on nodding terms with, hurried to join us.

'Well did you get Alcatraz or wherever it was you wanted them to send you?'

'Portland? No, I asked for it but they thought I'd be better off at Gaynes Hall, more suitable they reckon.'

'Well I'm going there as well so you won't be alone.'

We were taken to a shed in the grounds that seemed to have been some kind of after thought when the prison had been built. We were made to stand outside in the freezing cold with the rain trying very hard to have a go at pouring down. One by one we were led inside where cameras and lights cluttered up everywhere you moved.

Click, flash, bang, wallop, in no time I had been sat in a chair whilst a chalkboard with my name and number came just below my chest. Before I knew it they'd taken both front and profile shots and I was being hustled out of the shed back to the freezing outdoors with the others who were still waiting to join the family album. When the last frame had been exposed, the last face captured for all eternity we were led back to the relative warmth of our cells, at least it was better than the rain.

So,back to war in the jungle story, with someone going down with a serious case of Beriberi.

I passed on having tea as well, except I did go down for a brew, but no food, still wasn't quite up to it.

Time was creeping by so slowly.

At seven p.m all the cells on my landing were opened, we were told we to have one hour of association. That meant we could all go downstairs to the recreation area to play, darts, snooker, watch TV and generally mix with the other lads on the landing. I would have preferred to stay in my cell, mixing with the others still didn't really appeal to me.

I wasn't really a darts or snooker player so settled down to watch a far from interesting programme on the forth-coming decimalisation of our currency, then I wouldn't need to speak to anyone.

Most of the cons were chatting and laughing, I didn't speak a word until the guy sitting a few places to my left lent over to say something.

'Want a burn mate?'

'Yeah, thanks,' I was surprised at the friendly voice, 'I wouldn't mind one at all.' He passed me a thinly rolled cigarette and gave me a light off his.

'Have you been allocated yet?'

'Yes, Gaynes Hall, how about you?'

'I'm here for re-allocation, I've already done three months at Gaynes Hall myself but they shipped me back here for my own safety.' He looked around quickly to see that no one else was listening to him. 'Look' he pulled up is sleeve to reveal scores of razor cuts, all the way up his arm, 'that's what the bastards there did to me.' There were far too many for me to count before he rolled his sleeve down again. A shiver ran right down my spine and my body went cold at the thought.

'What, Gaynes Hall, but I thought?'

'What, you thought it was some kind of holiday camp?' he shook his head violently, 'far from it mate, believe me, they're a serious bunch of nasty bastards, just make sure you don't get into Jupiter house, that's where I was.

Give them my regards when you see them, say I'll get every one of the shit bastards when I get out, tell 'em Tim Ryan said so.'

There was a kind of emptiness in his eyes, like he was on drugs, a bit like his body was sitting in front of me but his mind was elsewhere. I was speechless, I could feel myself getting sweaty around my neck, I didn't like what I had heard one little bit. Before I had any chance to question him further the call for us to return to our cells came and he was gone in a flash.

As I waited for supper to come round I couldn't stop thinking very deeply about what mister Tim Ryan had told me. I wasn't sure what to think as it conflicted considerably with what I had already heard about Gaynes Hall. It made me feel very, very uneasy, those razor cuts were real enough, maybe he had been exaggerating a little.

Maybe.

My nodding acquaintance from the kitchen, I later discovered his name was Davy, brought around the supper that evening so my cake was somewhat larger than usual, he was a good lad. The tea was welcomingly warm and I was getting used to the idea of not having sugar in it. In fact, it even tasted a bit better.

I finished the book on jungle warfare just before the lights went out. I was even less sleepy than previous nights; the razor cuts were still very fresh in my mind.

It was another long night.

+++++++++++++++++

Saturday was a bit of a non-day really, except for the film, not much of a film to write home about but once again better than solitarily twiddling my thumbs my cell. So after lunch there was a mass exodus to a makeshift cinema where we saw a few cartoons for openers.

Then the main feature, about bees, very interesting it was but I would have preferred something a bit lighter. Still I learnt a lot about bees that day and it was warmer in the cinema than the cell so I sat back and made the most of it.

All good things, however, have to come to an end and that afternoon was no exception to that rule. It was dark when we left the comfort of the cinema so I guessed it had to be past five o'clock. That was the trouble you never really knew what time of day it was except by meal times and lights out. After those it was a matter of guessing, then you were generally wrong as the time dragged so much, a minute could seem like an hour.

I lay back on my bed waiting for Saturday to come to an end; I'd finished the jungle warfare book the night before and didn't really feel like starting another one.

I was fucking bored.

So bored that I started reading the walls that were covered in mementos, left by the many previous tenants in the form of colourful inscriptions. I felt that I would be failing in my role as a prisoner if I didn't leave my mark as well. I didn't really want to write verse or scribble my name with a biro; it had to be something more permanent and better than the rest.

I took my razor and with the corner proceeded to gouge my name into the metal of the door. Even when the door would be painted over, I thought to myself, my name will still be seen.

Immortal.

By lights out I had finished my name so I decided to add the date in the morning.

I wonder if it's still there?

++++++++++++++++

With Sunday morning came the ancient ritual that all institutions persist on inflicting to all and sundry no matter what your religious preferences.

Church.

Despite my admitted atheism I was forced to trot along with the rest of the cheery mob to the coldest pews this side of the Pope's kneeling block. I guess the others were probably glad of the break, I would have been happy to stay in my cell where I just wanted to continue with my etchings. Still I had to sit through 'Onward Christian Soldiers' and a few others mixed with prayers. Up and down from our knees like yoyo's we were.

Then,

The Sermon.

Groan.

There should be a statutory time limit for sermons; the few I have been forced to sit through have always seemed to go on for hours and hours.

This one was no exception.

The Devil dodger droned on and on, about what I couldn't possibly tell you, I wasn't listening; I tried without much success to sleep, to block out his boring voice.

At last he finished, we sang and prayed a bit more then, much to my relief, the weeks punishment was over. I feel that's the real purpose of things like that, to make life just that little bit more unbearable.

I was glad to get back to the cell again; it didn't take long to finish my etching on the back of the door so I started my last book. A murder mystery this time, which I managed to become quite engrossed in, so didn't really notice the time slipping away.

Having once again passed on lunch, I was feeling surprisingly hungry by teatime so I tried a little of the beans and Soya sausage. I immediately regretted my courage, as it was food most foul, so I settled for a slice of bread with a cup of tea.

Roll on supper.

It did, eventually, as well as lights out some two hours later as I was coming towards the end of my book, which I looked forward to finishing in the morning.

I still had a number of dog ends to make one last cigarette so I set about rolling one in the semi light of the cell. Having successful lit up from the half match I took a deep draw, it tasted like the bottom of a barrel of tar. It was dreadful but that didn't stop me from finishing it, it was better than nothing.

I think it even helped me to get some sleep that night.

++++++++++++++++

Not long after breakfast the next day the door to the cell swung open once more.

'Gray, get your kit together.'

'This is it,' I thought 'I'm being moved up to the three's at last.

'Then get your arse downstairs, you're moving out.'

So soon? I didn't wait to be told again, I had it packed in no time at all and was scurrying down the stairs in no time. Sad that I hadn't finished the book but I would get to finish it one day, I wanted out of there more.

I sat waiting patiently with a hoard of others until a screw came along with a clipboard. He read out the names of everyone else who was there, but not me, a mistake he said. It seemed like I wasn't going out that day after all, so it was back up to the cell to unpack.

Well, at least I'd get to finish the book.

So I settled back into good old 2/64 and got down to the last chapter of my book. Until, oh no some funny bastard had torn the back few pages out, to play battleships with no doubt. Now I knew how Tony Hancock felt with his 'Lady Don't Fall Backwards.'

More than a little annoyed!"

Still, Tuesday was another day.

+++++++++++++++

'Get your kit packed up and take it downstairs, you're being moved out today.' It was the same screw who had given me the news the day before.

'Are you sure this time, before I do that? I mean I don't want to have to come and…..'

'Less of your lip, just do it.'

'Gladly,' once more I packed up my kit and trundled it down to the main gate of the block. This time my name was on the list so I handed over the library books and pointed out the missing pages of the murder mystery. 'If you ever find out who did that be sure to write and let me know.'

We were led back across to where we had first arrived; there were twelve of us in all. I looked around at the faces; I hadn't seen any of them in the wing. They didn't seem anything like as sinister as the others had, perhaps I'd only imagined they'd been sinister. I was surprised not to see Davy from the

Kitchens as he had told me that he had been allocated to Gaynes Hall as well.

We only made small talk as we changed back into our own civilian clothes. I was glad to see the back of my baggy pants and over sized shoes and get back into something more familiar.

There were two officers in plain clothes from Gaynes Hall waiting to load us onto the bus that would take us to our new home. I was surprised to see that there were no bars on the windows this time. I sat down next to a lad who looked as if his hair was going grey already. We didn't speak much to start with but became quite chatty after he gave me a smoke, everyone else seemed to have burn but me, never did understand that one. The bus started to move out the gates on our long journey to Hertfordshire. Remember this was in the days before the M25 so the trip from West London to Hertfordshire took us through many places.

Ten days I'd been in the Scrubs, it had felt like ten months with Lord above knows how much more to go.

I wasn't sure if I would be able to handle it without cracking up.

One of the friendly looking officers stood up and handed us all a printed booklet. I looked at the cover.

'Welcome to Gaynes Hall.' It said

I just couldn't stop laughing.

* * * * *

Chapter Two
Good Morning Campers

The bus ride seemed to take hours, well it probably did, as I've already said, West London to Hertfordshire in 1971 didn't include a ride around the M25 to the A1(M) going north. The atmosphere during the journey had been very cordial indeed. I think we were all somewhat relieved to be getting away from the depression that had been Wormwood Scrubs. I'd been lucky to have only spent ten days there, a couple of my fellow travellers had been waiting for over three weeks to be transferred.

It was still daylight when I caught my first glimpse of the sign that stood at the entrance to 'H.M.B Gaynes Hall'.

There were no walls, no fences, no high metal gates, no bars and no barbed wire, just a group of single story buildings spread across the countryside. My first impression was that they looked a bit like an army camp or a very badly laid out Butlin's holiday camp. The bus pulled up outside these building's, one of which we were herded inside to discover the dining room and kitchens. The somewhat refreshingly pleasant office indicated that we should take a seat.

Trays were brought out to us, with what looked like real food on them.

Real food!

I hadn't eaten properly for ten days, granted mainly because I was so freaked out by my situation but also because what was dished up looked far from edible. Admittedly what lay before me wasn't quite up to the same standard as mum's home cooking but I ate every scrap there was.

Everything seemed to be quite informal, no screws shouting for you to get a fucking move on. In fact the two officers who had been on the bus were leaving us to eat, drink and chat amongst ourselves.

Eventually when everybody had finished we were taken, at a leisurely pace, to the hospital building. Very modern it seemed as well, complete with surgery, dentist's chair, waiting room and a ward with sixteen beds. We sat in the waiting room to see both a doctor and a dentist.

The reception orderly, who was also an inmate was introduced to us by the reception officer, Jim Hunt, as Dave Knight. Dave was due for release in four weeks time and this was a plum, nice and cushy job for the duration.

We all wanted to know the same thing.

'How long have you been here?' somebody asked him.

'Eight months, I'll have done nine by the time I leave here next month.' I was amazed; it now seemed possible to be out in less than the minimum year that I was expecting. 'The longest I've known anyone to here is fourteen months and you have to be pretty bad to do that long. Eight or nine months is about the average, four months on your red tie, two on the green and four to six weeks on the brown.'

The seniority system at Gaynes hall revolved around ties and their colour. There were four, blue for the new arrivals, receptions or 'Recepos', us, as we were affectionately known. Normally you would spend no more than four weeks on this tie. You would then be promoted to 'Training Grade' and sport a red tie in place of the blue. This was traditionally the longest serving colour, with a minimum time required of three months whilst the longest could be untold.

Every month there was a 'tie board' consisting of house officers and course staff. They would discuss your progress and if you had pushed the right buttons and were up for promotion they may well reward you.

The next such reward was the green tie or 'Senior Training Grade'. This would bring you a huge step closer to your discharge date, so, a short home leave of six days was granted which would take place six or eight weeks after the promotion to STG. The minimum length of time you could spend on this tie was one month but again, you could spend considerably longer. I do know of one guy who spent five months on his, but he was an exception. Generally by the time you reached green you were on your way out.

The last was the discharge or brown tie. If you were lucky enough to get it after only one month on the green you would know your release date when you went on home leave. Most would spend an average of four months on red and two on green. There was always the temptation, when you didn't have a release date, not to return from your home leave. However, in all the time I was there only one failed to return.

After my experiences with the doctor in the Scrubs I wasn't expecting a great deal from this one. I was wrong; each new arrival had a long chat with him. He was already aware of my having recently had tuberculosis of the lungs; at least the previous quack had been listening, I'd only been given the all clear a year before. He said that I shouldn't be doing any heavy physical work so I was classed as grade two labour. This was followed by and eye test, then over to the dentist chair where all my teeth were examined and X rayed. I hadn't actually been to a dentist since I left home so was quite relieved to find out later that I need no treatment.

Everybody seemed pleased, I wondered if this was some kind of softening process before the tough stuff started.

I would have to wait and see wouldn't I?

We spent quite some time at the hospital while each of us went through the routine. When the last one had been looked over we were led back past the canteen to the library. It wasn't that grand, in fact it was about half the size of my old school library, the chairs were comfortable though. Here we would go through the process of being booked in.

Jim Hunt went through all the usual questions, name, date of birth, religion, rank and serial number etc.

'Can you drive?' he asked me

'No,' came the honest reply but I saw him write down yes on the form. 'Excuse me, I said I can't drive,' I dutifully pointed out; he looked up at me and smiled.

'All Borstal Boys can drive when they're absconding.' I wondered why he bothered to ask.

'And what did you do before coming here?'

'I was a musician.' I replied

'Well I'm sorry to say there aren't many openings for musicians here. However, we do run courses in bricklaying, motor mechanics, electronics, business studies and cooking with a final exam in City and Guilds. How about one of those?'

'Not excited.' I answered

'No matter, you don't have to decide now, give it a couple of days thought. The Governor will be asking you the same question when you see him so have an answer ready for him.'

It would be the same, I said to myself.

After I'd signed the hotel register I was taken next door into the stores where I changed out of my civvies for the last time. Thankfully more trouble was taken to make sure that all the clothing I had came close to fitting properly. Also, all the items handed over to me were in pretty good condition then tied up inside my bed cover, like a larger version of Puss in Boots, for easy transportation.

After waiting until each one of us had completed the registration process, which once again took quite some time, and collected our kit, we returned to the library. It was now dark outside, winter evenings and all that.

Jim Hunt came back into the room.

'Each one of you will have a sponsor, another Borstal Boy, who will help ease your way into the way we do things here. You will be their responsibility for the next two weeks. They will show you the ropes, what you can and can't do, after that you'll be on your own so listen and learn. We're just waiting for them now.'

One by one the sponsors came to take their charges away to our separate dormitories. It was like being back at school with house, I was due for Jupiter house; there were two others, Neptune and Ariel. All ancient Gods, I hoped at least one of them was looking after me.

Mike Martin, my sponsor, was a big fella with a heavy five o'clock shadow that covered most of his face, one of those unlucky men who really needed to shave at least twice a day. He came for me after most of the others had gone. I was surprised at how friendly he was, picking up my kit to carry it over to the dorm. There were three of us going over to the same house so we all walked along together. One was a short stocky Scotsman and the other a beefy ginger headed guy who looked as if he'd be at home on a building site.

We exchanged a few words as we made our way across the camp to Jupiter house.

'What's this place like?' I asked Mike.

'Fucking holiday camp really,' he replied 'as long as you behave yourself it's a piece of cake.'

'How long have you been here?'

'Just coming up for my green, it's been three months on my red.' At this point I didn't know about the tie system so I innocently asked the question

'Do you think you'll get it?'

'Nah, I'm on the motor mechs' course and that's got another four months to run so they wont give it to me till next month, I'm not bothered really, at least I'll have a trade to go out with.'

I had already decided that a six-month course was not what I wanted to do.

In no time we arrived at the dormitory, Jupiter three or J3 for short, inside were fourteen beds, seven down each side and facing each other. The floor was a highly polished wood, which made you afraid to step on it. There were a number of inmates sitting on their beds who turned to stare at us as we came in. Then voices started raising to show us how tough they were as we were just the 'recepos'.

'Take your shoes off, always take them off before entering any dorm, we have to keep the centre deck shining, so, no shoes or boots.'

Obediently the three of us removed our shoes.

The beds didn't look very inviting, instead of springs there were metal straps going across. Although some beds had springs but you had to wait your turn to get one.

Mike told me to leave my kit on the bed until after we' been to tea, so I did just that and the entire dorm marched all the way back to the canteen. The procedure for obtaining food was weird and wonderful, every day each house took turns to go in first so that everyone had a crack at first choice. We had to wait for Neptune to finish, as Jupiter was second up on this day. Everyone's name was checked off on the role of honour as we passed through the door.

'Ah we have some recepos' beamed the Bob Lewis, the officer checking the names as we came in, 'and whom do we have here?'

'Kris Gray.'

'House and dorm?'

'Jupiter three.'

'Welcome young Gray.' He smiled, I passed through to take my tray and collect some food. Like the lunch we had on arrival, the food didn't seem too bad at all. It appeared that some kind of care had gone into its preparation. Still there were nowhere near as many to cater for here as there had been in the Scrubs and that helped.

Everyone sat hunched over their tables, some were talking, a few even laughing, but they all looked tired. The atmosphere of doom and gloom that had been prevalent in the Scrubs wasn't present. I didn't get the feeling of anger that I had felt there but still some tension was in the air. Mike seemed a little bit on edge but Gingers little Welsh sponsor was bubbling over with verbal diarrhoea.

Over our cup of tea we exchanged our reasons for being thrown together in these new surroundings. Mike had been caught breaking into a shop; he didn't say what kind of shop or what he was after. He did say that he hadn't done anything like it before and was shocked to get a Borstal sentence on his first offence. He was almost twenty-one, his said that his wife came to see him regularly but I could tell there was something else eating away at his insides.

Jupiter house was some distance from the rest of the Borstal buildings and it was soon time to make our way back.

'We're so isolated over here it's just like being in a completely different Borstal,' Mike quipped, 'even some of our rules are different from the others.'

No sooner had we arrived back at the dormitory and I was just about to unpack my kit when the door opened and another officer came in.

'All recepos go to Matron's office now.'

'You'll love 'er,' Mike chipped in.

Each house had a Matron who was supposedly there to look after our interests, a kind of motherly figure. The four Jupiter house recepos Jock Redding, Ginger Bates, Paul Masters and my good self sat in the small office as she beamed a smile at us.

'I want you to be able to look upon me as a friend, someone who you can talk to at any time about anything. No matter what problems you may be having. I'm here to listen. We can't assess what kind of a person you are or how long you should stay if you don't talk to us. So, we encourage you to do just that.

I help run the domestic side of life here, there's a savings bank for you to save towards your home leave, you must have at least ten shillings (a lot of money in those days) saved before you can go. I can also sell you cards for birthday, anniversaries, that sort of thing, as well as treating you or minor cuts and grazes.

We normally send a letter out to your families to inform them of your whereabouts, but with this postal strike looking to be going on for some time we will need telephone numbers to call them.

Visits are a lot more free and easy here, regulations state thirty minutes every month but we allow one every weekend. That can be on either Saturday or Sunday but not both. They start at midday and finish at five, if your visitors arrive on time you can be with them for five hours.

They are allowed to bring you food, drinks, non-alcoholic of course, and cigarettes. All these items are allowed to be consumed in the visiting room but not brought out and taken back to your dorms.

Girlfriends must have written parental consent for you to be able to write to them or before they can come to visit you.'

I didn't like the sound of that.

'Is there no room to move on that?' I asked 'my girlfriend and I have been living together for over a year now. Her mother lives in Scotland, seems unnecessary to tell her something she doesn't really need to know.'

'So she is your common law wife?'

'Yes.'

'I'll have a word with Mr Hawkes the housemaster.'

'Thank you.'

'OK boys, that's all for now, I know the library isn't all that well stocked but I do have a few paperbacks here if any of you would like to borrow for now, please help yourselves.'

The other three declined but I spotted a copy of 'Catcher in the Rye', which I had heard was a great book so gladly took it with me.

Just as we were about to leave, Bob Lewis came back in again to tell us our dorms had been changed. Jock and Ginger were to be moved over to J4, where Paul was already, whilst I went alone to J1. I wasn't all that enamoured with the idea of being the only new boy going into that dorm but it seemed that I would have no choice.

I went back to J3 to collect my kit where there was a tall blond guy waiting for me with a few others. He kind of leered and smiled at me all at the same time, I felt that he was someone you didn't mess with.

'OK recepo, I'm Alan Welch your new sponsor.' He put his hand out and a firm shake was made, I hate it when people shake like it was a dead fish but there was power in this guy's grip. 'We have to take the bed as well as there isn't one for you in ours.'

Two of the other lads picked up the bed and whisked it out the door in a flash. Alan grabbed my kit and beckoned me to follow as my new entourage marched out before me. Once inside the new dorm smiles and a much easier atmosphere than I had left, greeted me. A number of hands flew about making up my bed and laying out my kit for me in the way that it should be,

'Want a burn?' I turned around to see a smiling face behind a pair of the thickest spectacles I'd ever seen, he was holding a ready rolled cigarette out towards me, 'Chris Anderson, welcome aboard the good ship Jupiter One.'

'Thanks, I'm Kris as well, Kris Gray.' I took the cigarette gratefully and accepted a light from his. 'Been here long?'

'Ten months.'

'Sounds like a long time,' I quickly noted his green tie, 'no discharge date yet then?'

'Anderson's a bird man mate,' came a voice from the other end of the dorm,' he'll do his full term, just you see.'

'Piss of Coles!' Anderson spat back, then turned towards me again, 'screws reckon they don't know enough about me coz I won't go and talk to them, so they keep putting me off. I've had home leave but no sign of a discharge date.'

'They just don't like poofs old son.' Welch slapped him on the back whilst giving out a deep, dirty laugh.

'You can piss off too Welch, why don't you leave me alone, I don't go on at you all the time.'

'Pack it in you two,' a voice came from behind me, I turned to see a small guy coming towards me, 'don't take any notice of them, everybody winds Anderson up, leaves himself wide open, don't you Chris? Anyway, we like a bit of peace and harmony in this dorm. I'm Pete James, dorm leader, and it's my job to keep the peace. So come and sit down and tell us all about yourself, one of the rules here is no more than two on a bed,' we both sat on my bed and the others stood around or sat on the bed next to mine.

'So where are you from?'

'Originally from Romford in Essex but I've been living in Earls Court, in London, for the past year.'

'What you in for?' Oh no not again, I thought, and it wouldn't be the last time I told the story, I suspected that over the coming months I would relate it over a hundred times.

'I'm from Dagenham,' a hand thrust itself at me and we shook. 'Steve Waller, Romford ain't too far from me.' He definitely had the accent to go with it.

'I know,' I answered, 'I was born in Barking and my grandfather lives in Dagenham.'

'Get away, small world ain't it?'

'So it seems, what part of Dagenham are you from?'

'Just off the Longridge Road, behind the Robin Hood.'

'The World seems to be getting smaller Steve, my grandad lives in Lodge Avenue, just opposite the Robin Hood backing onto Mayesbrook Park.'

'Know it well,' he replied.

Pete James got up and went back to his own bed to allow Steve to sit next to me, 'Two's up your burn,' he asked as I took another draw on the cigarette.

'Two's what?' I asked somewhat puzzled by the request.

'Two's up, it means half of what you've got, you share it with me, half your burn, food, book, newspaper, whatever, or 'after you' if you like. If I'm reading the dorm newspaper and you say 'two's up' then you get to read it next, get the idea?'

'I think so,' I replied and handed what was left of my cigarette over to him. This was a ritual that could become intensely annoying as the weeks and months went by but everyone adhered to it without complaint. We sat talking for some time before the officer on duty came round to tell me we had five minutes to lights out. That meant we all had to be in bed by the time he came back again to turn them off.

We were.

He reappeared with the night watchman who clocked himself in on his first round by the device that was on all dormitory walls. I was so surprised when the lights went out to leave red bulbs glowing right down the middle of the room; I hadn't expected that at all.

Nobody wore pyjamas, despite the fact that everybody had been issued with a pair,

'Only poofs wear pyjamas,' Welch pointed out. It wasn't a problem, I hadn't worn them since I'd been six years old, wanted to be just like my dad who never wore them either, still don't, can't bear clothes in bed.

I was sitting up in bed, not feeling particularly sleepy at the time. The guy in the bed facing me was sitting up as well, plucking the hair from his scalp, strand by strand, then looked up and spoke to me.

'Sorry, I didn't quite catch your name.'

'Kris, Kris Gray.'

'I'm Kevin Ross, welcome aboard.'

'Thanks,'

'So, what did you do on the out?'

'I was a musician,' he seemed to brighten up at that.

'Really? I play guitar, what about you?'

'Guitar and bass, bass mostly.'

'I was semi-pro, used to play in a Latin American show band.' Which wasn't my favourite kind of music, but never mind, having another muso around wasn't such a bad thing. We would become firm friends despite his lack of musical taste, something I would tease him with mercilessly.

Inevitably we finally got around to what had brought us both to this place. I went through my, by now, well-worn story, then he told me his sad tale. He had been working in the accounts department of a large building firm. One day a discrepancy had appeared revealing a large sum of money being unaccounted for. Unfortunately the finger of blame pointed quite squarely at Kevin. As we spoke about it he was awaiting the hearing of his appeal. He told me that he was innocent, another one, and that he knew who the real culprit was. He was even allowed to have all the paperwork at Gaynes Hall to enable him to look over the evidence and prove his case.

I remember the day he went to the court, dressed in his suit, to hear the appeal. I so felt for him when he returned with the news that the appeal had been denied and he would have to complete his sentence.

I don't think the appeal helped with his passage through Gaynes Hall, nor anyone else who tried the same thing. He might have spent a bit longer there than he would have had he just bitten the bullet and done his bird, quietly. Even now I'm not sure if I believed he was innocent, I know that nobody else in our dorm did. But then the whole prison system is full of innocent people isn't it? It didn't stop us becoming firm friends.

Talking finally petered out and I eventually drifted into a heavy, dreamy sleep.

+++++++++++++++

That heavy, dreamy sleep was soon over as I was brought back to earth with a bump as the lights were turned on and the voice of Bob Lewis boomed out.

'All right me lad's, wakey, wakey, time to get yourselves on the move, up and out of bed, come on.'

It was six o'clock, bitterly cold and very dark outside, it was so cold I was afraid to prise myself from between the sheets to get out of bed.

'Come on Kris,' came the growling voice of Alan Welch 'I'll show you where the bath house is.' I leapt out of bed and threw my clothes on as quickly as I could to follow him out into the black morning. 'When you get your first visit, tell them to bring you some soap, toothpaste and things like that, the stuff they give you here's no good at all. Until then you're welcome to share mine.'

Despite his somewhat rough exterior, Alan seemed to be all right on the inside.

We were expected to shave everyday, whether we needed to or not, no growth of any kind was allowed at all, either on the face or the head. Haircuts were administered every two weeks by a civilian barber who was as kind to ones appearance as he could be, given his remit for the job.

Sideburns were definitely not allowed, the ruling was, and that depended on what officer you were with, recepos shouldn't have any; they stopped at the top of your ears. Some officers might let them creep down a bit but certainly no lower than mid ear. TG and STG might be ok mid ear but no longer, discharges were allowed to take them to the ear lob but anything further than that was definitely a no, no!

After the morning ablutions were complete Alan took me over to breakfast where he told me of his associations with the Hells Angels. He came from Croydon in Surrey, as did Alan Mitchell who was also in J1. They had been friends on the outside, it was very rare for two people who knew each other to be in the same Borstal let alone the same dorm. Welch told me that he had been one of 'the biggest Angels in the area. I found it hard to imagine a chapter of the Hells Angels ripping up downtown Croydon, in those days the idea of the Hells Angels and England didn't really go together, more wannabes than anything else.

However, he was now a fallen Angel.

'I had really long hair before I came in here,' Welch told me 'right down to my chest, and I've got a 750 Harley Davidson waiting for me when I get back.'

I very quickly came to realise that not everything people inside told you was true. Maybe there was always a seed of truth in the story, they would just elaborate it to make them sound a lot more interesting than just plain crooks. Maybe Alan was telling me the truth, maybe he did have a big bike, and it was good to believe him at the time. There wasn't much else to do but swap yarns, even if they were a little on the tall side. I have to confess I used to talk up my musical career a bit, which would one day cause me some pain, but that comes later.

After breakfast we returned to the dorm to put on our overalls ready for work. The reception party would do whatever menial task they were set and in between those we would visit vocational officers, governors and more. All of us who had arrived together the day before would stay together for two weeks before being moved on to whatever job or course we were assigned to.

I could hear murmurs going around the rest of the dorm about fire extinguishers.

'No!' came Pete's firm voice, he then came over to me. 'Some dorms play tricks on their recepos, like telling them that they have to take the fire extinguisher on parade for inspection. It may seem funny but it reflects on the dorm leader, so I won't do it, anyway we aren't that childish, are we lads?' he said as he glanced around the room at everyone.

'No,' came the stern reply.

It was a very cold morning and we had no warm coats, only a blue denim like jacket. We all stood huddling in groups until the officers came with the call to get on parade. Alan showed me where the reception party had to line up, everybody had their own positions to line up in depending on what work party or course they were on.

'Come on you lot get on parade' barked the voice of Bob Lewis as everyone shuffled into position. 'Parade, parade attenshun!'

We new boys quickly got the idea and formed a line where we stood. All the officers had arrived on the scene by now, each one to a party. Jim Hunt was our officer; he wandered around us making sure that we'd all shaved and was properly dressed for the occasion.

'Parade, parade stand at ease!' The wind was whistling through my bones and I wondered how long we would have to stand there. Slowly Bob Lewis went through the role call, the fact that there had been one at breakfast was immaterial, and role calls were a fact of life that happened constantly all day. One hundred and eighty names take a long time to get through and it would seem even longer in the freezing wind.

Eventually it came to an end.

'All right, lead off!' one by one the various groups made their way to wherever they needed to be, we stood waiting until all the others had gone, daylight was breaking at last.

'Right then lads,' Jim smiled at us,' before we get down to some work we'll go over to the shop where you can get your allowance of reception tobacco.' That was a blessing, to be able to have something of my own to smoke at last. Although it wasn't much, a quarter of an ounce in fact, it came in very handy indeed. As we all now had some, except Ginger who didn't smoke, there would be no poncing of smokes. After celebrating our good fortune with a cigarette all round, we returned to the parade ground where morning had finally arrived in all its glory.

Jim Hunt was waiting for us.

'Now, I want you all to go back to your dorms, you six fetch a broom while the rest of you fetch a bumper.' Bumpers were used to polish the wooden floors, every morning footprints had to be removed before we all went to work. Dorms had to be clean and tidy at all times, everybody's kit had to be neatly laid out. I had to fetch a bumper and they weren't all that easy to carry, especially as we had to march at the same time.

We had to march everywhere we went, this morning we were to march all the way to the officer's mess, not a short distance, especially with the heavy bumper.

All the officers and their families lived on site in a small housing estate where they had their own social club in which to entertain themselves. There wasn't that much to do in that part of the country, only the small village of St Neots nearby and Huntingdon a small town a little further away.

Our job for the day was to clean the main clubroom, polish brass window handles and the toughest job was to bumper the wide expanse of flooring. This entailed getting down on one's hands and knees, to rub the polish into the wood with a piece of rag. Then, when it had dried, use the bumper to take it off, leaving a dull sheen behind. Then a large cloth was attached to it for a second work over that would leave it shining. Hunt made us do this twice more until he was satisfied when the result, more likely until we had killed enough time before lunch.

We were told to report after lunch in our best clothes, grey trousers instead of the overalls, dark blue jacket instead of the work jacket, and our ties. No work was to be done in the afternoon; instead we were taken on a guided tour of all the courses and various jobs in the establishment. First stop were all the courses, these buildings were all grouped together.

There was the motor mechanics course, which I didn't fancy at all. I'd worked in a petrol station as a Saturday job when I was at school and found the grease a little too much for me. This one, like all the others, had a duration of six months but didn't start again or another two which would mean I'd have to stay for at last nine months and I was determined to get out long before that. There were three from my dorm there and I received knowing nods from them as I passed through.

The instructor gave us his sales talk as to why we should join this course, it all sounded very attractive but I had already decided to fight against the whole idea of courses. Never the less I had to complete the tour, which included almost choking on brick dust in the brickies shop. Alan Welch was there, this seemed like the best course, when it was finished if you weren't on discharge there was a chance of doing outside work. This sales gimmick still had no effect on my good self, my mind was made up, I would angle to get myself on to the farm.

The tour continued peacefully till the end of the day with a chat from the electrical engineering instructor and business studies man. You were not allowed on that course if you had been convicted of any kind of fraud, like cooking the books. Poor Kevin had wanted to do it but had instead been relegated to swill boy on the farm. It sounded like a shit job but it had distinct advantages like working alone and unsupervised, a trusted position.

+++++++++++++++

That evening I was introduced to the Entertainments Committee, of which Kevin was a member. So, due to the fact that I could play a few tunes on an instrument or two he asked me if I would like to come along and join the gang. The idea certainly appealed to me for a number of reasons, the main one being that it would mean I would get to bring one of my guitars in. the second would be that I would be able to go places outside of Gaynes Hall.

We went along to a meeting in one of the classrooms where I met two other members of the committee. I'm not sure what I was expecting but Brian Johnston and Andre Wilson didn't fit the picture. Johnston was definitely a strange dude, these days he would be diagnosed as having an obsessive, compulsive disorder. Like most people who suffer from this he was obsessed with cleanliness. His clothes had to be immaculate.

He was, unfortunately, in the wrong place for that.

Clean clothes were only issued once a week, twice for underwear and socks and Brian would complain bitterly. He would bath everyday, not something most of us did and would wash his hands and face at once every hour. He never struck me as the criminal type and I don't think I ever found out what he was in there for. Despite his mental impediment he was a nice easygoing guy who I had no trouble rubbing along nicely with.

Andre Wilson was a chirpy little guy who had one leg shorter than the other and was referred to by everyone as 'Peg leg'. He claimed to be an actor and would perform recitations and monologues, even a little Shakespeare. He would sadly turn out to be quite useless at both of those things but quite good at organising everyone else to do their bit. Benny King was the officer in charge and who had such high hopes for us. Considering his lofty position, Benny was quite a friendly character and would treat us like human beings.

There was an upcoming gig for us in a couple of weeks at an old folks home, this posed a bit of a problem; before I could have my guitar sent in I had to make a Governor's request, but I couldn't make one of those until I had been promoted to a red tie. To make matters more complicated the tie board was the day after the gig and there was no other guitar to be found in there.

Benny said he would see what he could do to bend the rules.

We discussed some kind of programme for the evening, which would include a couple of songs from me and a couple from Kevin. Brian had said that he could play some drums but the kit they had for him was so bad the idea had to be abandoned. Instead it was decided that he would perform some comedy sketches with Andre to help pad the evening out.

The meeting disbanded at nine so that we could go to supper, which, like the Scrubs, consisted of a piece of cake and a steaming mug of tea. Over this Kevin and I, joined by the two Alans from J1, discussed people we knew and had played with in the world of music. Kevin's musical tastes were vastly different to mine; well he had played with a Latin American band. Once he absolutely slaughtered the Beatles Norwegian Wood by playing a la Edmundo Ross, yuk!

Kevin was a bit of an anomalous person; he looked considerably older than he said he was. I placed him at maybe even thirty but he swore that he was only twenty. Everyone used to pull his leg about his age, we all thought the same thing. Borstal was for young offenders up to the age of twenty-one, over that and you went to prison. It was widely believed that he reduced his age because he might have received a longer prison sentence had he been over twenty-one and Borstal was a safer bet.

In that respect, he was right.

He never admitted to being older, right up to the day he went out.

That night, back at the dorm and lights out I was introduced to a dubious piece of dormitory entertainment known at 'The Boat Vote'. It was always played on one of the first few nights after a recepo had landed in the dorm.

The idea was simple, all of us in the dorm are in a lifeboat after a ship had sunk, however, there were too many in the lifeboat for it to stay afloat, so, to save it from sinking two people had to be thrown out. Each person in the dorm had a choice of who would be ejected, so we went around the room starting with the dorm leader.

'OK, I'll set the ball rolling and end up with Chris Saunders. Pete was silent for a few moments, 'not too difficult a choice, Cohen and Anderson.'

Now it was Phil Johnson's turn, I hadn't really spoken to him yet but despite the bad start we were to have we would become very firm friends before he went out.

'No, Anderson's all right, I'll chuck out Cohen and the recepo.'

I was surprised and hurt, not only because someone that I didn't really know was evicting me from the boat but also, by being referred to as 'The Recepo' rather than by my name. I later learnt not to take the boat vote seriously; it was standard procedure to throw out the new guy to put them in their place.

Now it was my sponsor Alan's turn

'Mitchell, and the recepo.' I began to sink below the sheets, although I knew Alan Mitchell was Welch's friend it still didn't occur to me that it was all a set up for my benefit.

Alan Mitchell took up the challenge.

'Well, after that Welch has just got to go!' A deep chuckle came from Welch's bed, I grew to know and love that sinister laugh very well. 'And let me see, ah yes Cohen.' I was beginning to realise that Russell Cohen was one of the dorm fall guys; the other one was Chris Anderson.

Now it was my turn, I didn't really know anybody so I just plumped or the two I thought wouldn't take it seriously.

'Kevin and Pete,'

'Cheeky bastard,' came Pete's voice as the whole dorm burst into laughter, it would seem that the dorm leader was very rarely thrown out. Even then it was usually by a friend as a joke.

Chris Anderson was in the next bed to me and despite the fact that most had picked on him he made an honest choice.

'Welch and Coles.' Gavin Coles was next to him, he was a giant and knew he didn't really have much to worry about from anyone else, accept maybe Welch. They seemed to have a healthy respect for each other because, I was certain, they weren't quite sure of each other's abilities in a straight fight. To show his disapproval of Anderson's choice his bony fist came over to thump him in the chest.

'Fuck you Coles!' Chris wheezed, everyone else laughed.

'You great big tart Anderson, if I could chuck you out twice I would and that dip stick front wheeler Cohen.'

Harry Norton was the strong silent type who lay in the corner bed on my side of the dorm. I was sure he could look after himself as well.

'Cohen and Coles.' Coles didn't hit him

In the opposite corner lay big Jim Groves, ready to go to the discharge unit in four weeks time and pretty much kept himself to himself.

'Anderson and the recepo.' I was beginning to feel as disliked as Cohen and Anderson. Sid Cohen was next, the dorm metaphoric punch bag, a little Jewish boy who everybody picked on, including, I'm sorry to say, myself. Well I did to start with because everyone else was but we would quickly become friends, especially when his girlfriend would come and visit with Moira.'

'Anderson and the recepo.' I guessed he'd chosen Chris and me to be on the safe side; anybody else probably would have punched his lights out. I think the one who disliked him the most was Gavin Coles and Russell was scared shitless of him.

Steve Waller, he of Dagenham fame chirped up next, he was known as the dorm reest, a word that meant someone who was, dirty, scruffy and untidy. Steve was a great guy but no matter what he did or how he dressed he was, without a doubt, a reest, he always looked like a tramp. Perhaps it was the Dagenham connection, you know, you take a boy out of Dagenham but......! We did become very good friends.

'Don't know why you're all picking on the recepo, he's all right by me so let's get rid of the creeps like Anderson and Cohen.' It would appear that I had a friend, a good one at that.

'I'd get rid of Coles and Ollie.' It was Kevin's turn

'You're a cunt Ross, I'd kick you out as well.' Coles certainly didn't like anyone to throw him out; he could be very childish really despite his tough guy image.

Ollie, Oliver Troughton, although he looked a little bit weak was far from it, came next. He sat in silence for a few moments considering carefully what he had to say.

'Well, logically speaking, the reason for discarding two people is to make the boat lighter, preventing it from sinking. Right? Therefore I propose the obvious choice, without any malice to those concerned, just pure logic, is Welch and Coles as they're the biggest.'

Everyone roared with laughter, Ollie certainly had a logical mind, although he didn't always apply it to the boat vote. Now last but by no means least came Chris Saunders, a long serving lad solely because he wouldn't talk to the staff, something I soon came to realise was a very important factor to getting out.'

'I suppose Ross really has to go, I'm not logical like you Ollie, and the Penguin' there was silence.

'Who?' asked Welch,

'Penguin, the recepo.' I really wished that I wasn't there; I knew what he meant it was because I had kipper feet but had never before been referred to as a penguin. I was stuck with that name for a long time before the novelty wore off.

Well, that was the boat vote, not the last time I would be ejected but it hurt a lot less on subsequent occasions. There were a number of variations like whose girl friend would you like to sleep with, favourite film stars and pop stars. Then there was the shoot and shag, again two names, one to shoot and one to shag but you never said which was which.

I was learning a lot about survival at Gaynes Hall, perhaps it wouldn't be that difficult after all.

++++++++++++++++

For the next few days our work activities consisted of moving a mound of earth from one end of a long track to fill in holes in the ground between the trees at the other end. It was obvious that they had nothing better for us to do. The ground was bloody hard so some of us used pick axes to loosen the frozen soil while the rest of us shovelled it up into the cart. Then we had to move it down the track, this was by no means an easy task. The tracks were frozen solid in places and horribly muddy in others. This, together with the weight in the cart made the moving of it somewhat arduous. It took anything up to an hour to move the whole load down the two hundred yards or so of track.

The easiest part of the job however came at the other end when all we had to do was unload the earth and spread it around. This part would take longer than necessary, deliberately of course, so that we could recover enough for the next load. Ginger, being built like the side of a house and twice as thick, took the lead in showing us all how it should be done. He even tried to move the cart on his own; it was a gallant effort that resulted in victory for the cart, which turned out to be even more stubborn than he was.

Paul Masters was a born shirker; he would manage quite easily to avoid hard, physical work as much as he could, quite successfully at that. This naturally annoyed the rest of us, including Ginger who eventually threatened him with a shovel, his pride was injured, and he worked just a hard as everyone else, he said.

It was during this period of work that we had the afternoon off to see the Governor. It was a blessed rest for us recepos, not that Jim Hunt and Dave Knight noticed, they would happily stand and watch us getting thinner every day. Sometimes Dave Knight would put his shoulder to the cart to help us out but his days of working hard were over.

That afternoon we were marched to 'The Big House', as the actual Gaynes Hall building was called. We had to wear our best bib and tucker to be interviewed by the Governor and his deputy. We all sat in the corridor with Dave Knight whilst Jim disappeared for a cup of tea in the office. Somehow the conversation came around to drugs, most of us admitted to having had a smoke or two and some, including myself owned up to dropping a tab of acid now and then, although I was sceptical of the truth being told. Ginger was violently against it as was Paul Masters but Nigel, who was in for possession, told me he used to deal from Earls Court. I was naturally curious having been doing very similar in the same area.

'I used to score most of my gear from two guys in Earls Court Square.' He told me after I had told him that I used to live there, then, when he mentioned the number I knew whom he meant. I'd scored from them as well. 'Will you see them when you get out?'

'I'm sure I will,' although I wasn't really sure at all.

'Tell them I'm ok, the last time they saw me was when the law were leading me away in handcuffs, they were looking a little horrified.'

'I used to smoke a bit of hash.' piped up 'simple' Simon Jones, as he soon became known because he wasn't the sharpest tool in the box. 'It were really good,' his thick Brummie accent grated on my ears. Nigel looked at him in a sorrowful way and spoke in his wonderfully soft Norfolk lilt.

'What did you get out of it then Si?'

'A foking good buzz.' He laughed.

'Is that all, you didn't get anything else out of it?' I asked

63

'No mate, just another good way to get bombed.' Both Nigel and I looked at each other, shaking our heads in disbelief. 'Why, do you take it for some other reason?'

'Sure,' Nigel answered 'it helps to develop awareness.'

'Do you really believe that crap?'

'Sure, it's done wonders for my spiritual self and my awareness has increased.'

'Ah Bollocks!'

I looked at Nigel and we both shrugged our shoulders, it wasn't worth trying to make him see our point of view, he was never going to see it.

The Governor was seeing us in alphabetical order, which meant that I was fifth in line. Heywood was the Governors name, a man in his late fifties with a gammy leg and a pigeon chest who also suffered from occasional attacks of malaria. I heard that he had been in a Japanese prisoner of war camp where he contracted the disease, he wasn't a bad guy.

Soon it was my turn to be called into his office.

'Sit down Gray,' he motioned to the chair in front of him.

He had a warm face and as I sat perched on the edge of the chair he smiled at me for a brief moment before looking back through my file without saying anything till he looked up.

'Are you settling in all right?' I nodded my head whilst giving him a faint yes. 'Good, good, so, now you have had a chance to see what we have to offer you in ways of self improvement, what do you think you might like to do?'

'Get out,' were the words in my mind but kept them to myself. 'I'd quite like to have a chance to work with the animals on the farm sir.' He looked at me for a few moments, as if sizing me up and turned back to my file.

'I think perhaps that would be a bit of a waste for you, it would seem that you are quite an intelligent lad and perhaps the business studies course would suit you much better.' I must have visibly winced, 'or at least one of the courses where you might make a better use of yourself instead of wasting your talents on the farm.'

'I have my reasons.'

'And may I ask you what they are?'

'Well, it should tell you in that file that I recently suffered from TB and have only just had a clean bill of health. Petrol fumes, brick dust and the like aggravate my lungs, apart from that, things like that aren't really me.'

'So what is 'really you'?'

'I'd really like to work with the animals.'

He looked at me or a few moments, trying to work out if I was pulling an elaborate hoax or not.

'I see, well we will consider this carefully when we come to allocating you to a work party.' He turned to Dick Clark, the deputy Governor, 'any questions Mr Clark?' He just shook his head.

'OK, that will be all for now, you will be seeing your housemaster at eight tonight, but I'm sure he will let you know that as well.'

I stood up and left the room.

+++++++++++++++++

That evening Ginger, Jock, Paul and I waited to see Ron Hawkes our Housemaster. He turned out to be quite a decent guy really, considering his job, we talked about my wish to go on the farm and it seemed as if he was supporting me in my request. He also told me that it would be alright for Moira to visit me and write without her mothers consent, he understood the situation. He also brought up the subject of my wanting to reconnect with a music career on the out. It was the first time that I thought they might not be too happy with that idea, something that would become a lot clearer in the weeks to come. A life of rock and roll was not thought to be something a rehabilitated Borstal Boy should be considering.

I didn't initially understand what the problem was, I mean not every rock musician ended up on the wrong end of the law. Perhaps it was the belief, probably quite rightly, in a lot of cases that it led to a life of drugs. However I realised that if I wanted to get out I had to play the game their way.

Friday was payday and I received the princely sum of 3/6d, decimalisation was literally around the corner. Britain would dump the old pounds, shillings and pence on the 15th February for the new system of one hundred pence to the pound and no shillings. That meant my 3/6d would become 17.5 new pence, just enough to buy a quarter of an ounce of tobacco, a packet of cigarette papers and a box of matches. Regulations stated that at no time were we allowed to have more than a week and a half's pay, in cash or kind. If you did, this would be classed as 'baroning' or profiteering from selling and that was a no, no.

I looked at my small packet of tobacco, knowing that it probably wouldn't last beyond the weekend, and rolled myself a pretty thin one. No one called out twos up, they all had enough of their own, it would be a few days before I would hear that called out.

That evening the reception party had an audience with the resident devil dodger, the Reverend Small who smiled sweetly at all of us and asked our religious denominations. As with all of Heaven's right hand men, he never batted an eyelid when I told him I had no religious beliefs. So the conversation went from the total believers through the not sure down to me who was, and still am, a firm non-believer.

He was a good conversationalist however, whilst trying very hard to make his case but I think he knew that he would never shift me towards becoming a believer. Of course the conversations came around to the subject of drugs, inevitable for a great many conversations we seemed to have in Borstal. This put Nigel and I in opposition over the subject, both of us had at one time been very heavily in the use of LSD. He professed that it had brought him even nearer to God, leaving him in no doubt that God was real.

I, on the other hand, pointed out that it was really a matter of deep down belief. As I hadn't believed in God since the age of nine years old my acid experiences only proved even more conclusively to me that there could be no God. He couldn't understand my logic but on the other hand I couldn't understand his either. Like all good arguments on the subject of religion or politics we agreed to differ and worship whom or whatever we wished, in his case God and in mine, John Lennon.

We left the devil dodger hoping to see us in church this coming Sunday, I promised he wouldn't see me.

+++++++++++++++

Every Saturday morning was a right, royal, organised pain in the proverbial arse. From the moment we were out of bed until 11am there was pandemonium beyond belief to prepare everything and everyone for the weekly inspection.

This entailed every inmate rushing about doing their own personal jobs as well as dorm chores. My job was to clean all the brass work, which included doorknobs, window handles and ashtrays, it was an easy task compared to some others, like cleaning the toilet. Everybody's kit had to be just right, all footwear had to shine so much that the glint could be used to flash Morse code. We had two pairs of boots, one for work and the other, well the other was just for show really. A pair of shoes to wear at the weekends and a pair of black gym shoes that also had to be polished.

The bed had to be stripped and a bed pack made up which meant that all sheets and blankets had to be folded neatly and placed in a pile at the head. The cover would be laid over the bed with the folded articles placed on top. The pillow was taken out of its case, which was also folded and placed on the pile.

The wooden floor that was my 'bed space' had to be polished in much the same way as we had in the officer's mess. It was the area that your bed stood on and the space next to it right up to the next bed. This area could change, depending on how many there were in the dorm. I was solely responsible for this piece of floor and it had to shine as much as, if not more than, my boots, if that were at all possible. This left what was known as 'the centre deck', this was the toughest of the dorm jobs and it was down to Alan Welch and whoever's turn it was to help him. Like the bed spaces it had to be smothered in brown polish then bumpered up to shine gloriously.

Each locker had to be tidy with no rubbish of any sort, no dog ends or scraps of paper were allowed. All clothes had to be neatly folded with block of wood placed inside to make them look so much neater. Above all no dust was to be in evidence either on the floor, windowsills or in lockers. The rubber feet on the beds were the biggest culprits for collecting dust so special attention was given to them.

When all the jobs were finished everyone had to change into their best clothes, always worn on the weekends, then wait outside for the inspection team to arrive. One week they would start with us and the other J4, when they were ready to inspect us we had to tip toe carefully to our bed space.

'J1!' boomed Pete's voice, somewhat like a drill sergeant, 'by your beds, J1, atten-shun!' we all stood to attention and stayed that way while Hawkes inspected us personally at first then looked over our bed spaces. He wasn't the hardest of inspectors but remarked on the length of the fingernails on my right hand. I grew them to enable me to finger pick the guitar,

'For picking your nose Gray?'

'No Sir, picking the guitar.'

'Sorry my lad but we can't have you scratching out someone's eyes with them now so I'm afraid they will have to go, nail scissors in the office after inspection.'

At least he has been quite nice about it.

After looking carefully the length and breadth of the dorm he managed to find just a small amount of dust; well we couldn't be totally perfect could we? Then complimented us on a job well done and left, everyone breathed a hefty sigh of relief. Most sat back on their beds and proceeded to roll up a smoke, including me.

'I wonder if we'll get the shield back this week?' Steve mused.

The shield was a prize that all four dorms in Jupiter house competed for every week; Neptune and Ariel also had one each. It was awarded to the cleanest and the smartest dorm of that week. J1 had lost it previously to J3, this grated with everyone as J3 were always known as the 'reest' dorm, the filthy one.

Now that the inspection was all over we could remake our beds then sit back and relax. I was about to stub out my smoke and put the dog end back into the tin Ollie had given me when Jim Hunt came in.

'You've done it again lads,' and handed the shield over to Pete where he hung it over his bed, 'keep it up!' he beamed a smile around the dorm and left.

'Never doubted it for a minute,' quipped Welch, without looking up from the cigarette he was rolling as the door closed behind Hunt.

Although in future I would rarely be present to enjoy the privilege of experiencing these rituals I would still have to endure the preparations which I would dread every week. Though for every winning dorm there had to be a loser whose prize would be, not the shield, but the honour of cleaning out the bathhouse and toilets for a week, something J1 did on a few occasions over the next few months.

Now it was time for us all to relax, it was the weekend, there was no work and we were wearing our best bib and tucker. After lunch I received the biggest surprise I could ever hope for, as I lay sprawled out on my bed the day officer came into the dorm.

'Gray, over to the visiting rooms, you've got a visit.'

It took a couple of seconds for what he said to sink in, a visit, it had to be mum and dad, Moira would have had a real problem getting there. I was elated and moved as quickly as I could over to the visiting rooms that were situated next to the main admin offices and classrooms. I had to report to the office first to check in and was then pointed in the right direction.

I walked in to find my parents, and, Moira.

This time I was smiling instead of crying, it was so bloody good to see them all. They had received the phone call to inform them of my whereabouts and were given permission to visit; in future I would have to make a request via a visiting order, VO. We had a pleasant few hours during which I told them all about life at Gaynes Hall, which made them, feel a lot better about my welfare. It was agreed that my parents would come on one weekend and Moira on the next; I knew it would be something I could to look forward to every week.

As they had arrived late this time we only had a couple of hours together, still, it was a couple hours more than I had expected and a lot longer than the Scrubs. They let me know that my grandfather and Moira's mother had been told that I had gone on a European tour with a band, I don't know if her mother believed it.

Mum had brought me a half-ounce of tobacco, which, officially I couldn't bring in but Keith Saunders was on tea duty and managed to smuggle it in for me for which I gave him a third of it. There would be much smuggling of contraband over the following months, some of which could have kept me there for a lot longer than the six till two I'd been sent there for.

As they were about to leave Moira handed me a letter that she had been writing since the day I had been sentenced. As the Royal Mail was on strike, and would be for many weeks to come, she couldn't post it. This letter and a few more that came by some of the many pirate postal services would be a lifesaver. Unfortunately although I could receive letters by these entrepreneurs I was unable to send any. Welch once said that he was going to kick the crap out of the first postman he saw when he was released, although I doubt that he ever did.

When the post finally got back to normal and we were able to send letters out, there was also a market in unofficial letters. These were uncensored and posted by either those out on home leave, discharges or outside workers, it wasn't easy getting one of these out, I managed it once, more about that later.

Moira handed in a letter for me and it was over twenty A4 pages long, in the future she would send letters of up to forty pages. This would sometimes cause problems with the officers who had to read them, some would just pass them without even reading it, others, well I did have a serious problem once, but that's another story for later.

Since I had been sent down Moira had been forced to move from our tiny flat in Richmond due to the fact that the rent was too high for her to keep up with alone. The landlady, Mrs Razamataz, as we used to call her, because we couldn't pronounce her name, became quite upset and managed to get away with keeping our sixty pounds deposit, not a small sum back in 1971, poor Moira had no idea how to handle the old witch.

+++++++++++++++

Sunday was a real drag; I slept most of it away when I wasn't reading. In the evening the house record player was allowed to make an appearance and a few decent records had an airing. Someone had Janis Joplin's new album 'Pearl' sent in, you were allowed to do that, so I listened to it closely having been a big fan since the Big Brother days. I never had any of my albums sent in, I was too possessive of them and couldn't have accepted even a minor scratch.

Coffee was also available at two pence a cup but I couldn't afford it this time round 17.5 new pence didn't go very far, even in those heady days of 1971!

Sundays were always a bore.

The days of the reception party dragged past slowly whilst we continued to shift our mounds of earth from pile A to pile B, most unrewarding. Then one afternoon we were taken along to the gym for our period of physical torture. I thought we had done enough of that by shovelling dirt but oh no there was more to come.

Never the less, these energetic cons threw themselves into the gym ready to work off even more calories. I was not keen; I had never been very good at climbing ropes and leaping over boxes and hadn't done so since before I had TB. Ginger was the first on the floor and leapt about like a maniac. Jim Hunt, who was supervising us at the time, decided that we would partake in a little circuit training. If you have never had the pleasure of this kind of physical torture, let me explain. It includes such medieval implements as a trampoline, monkey bars for climbing up, weights, ropes, boxes to jump over and Christ knows what else to almost kill you.

Once these evil devices were in place the idea was to go around the course three times spending two minutes at each position.

Simple.

A piece of the proverbial cake.

To the insane!

Or, in my opinion, if you were Superman, I thought I'd left all this shit behind when I left school, it was a bit like being back there with that arch bastard Pinder with whom I shared a mutual hatred. I completed the first circuit feeling somewhat nauseous by the time I had finished. I was not permitted to have a rest before being thrust into the second circuit. Less than half way around I realised that I had very little chance of completing the third. I had only just started number three when I couldn't see properly and half way through some press-ups I passed out.

Nobody seemed to notice me lying mumbling on my stomach, trying hard to fight my way back to consciousness. Eventually Ginger came over and lifted me back on to my shaky feet then sat me down on a bench.

'What's the matter chum, too much for you to handle?' I was afraid to nod in case I threw up all over him. Somehow I managed to get dressed and with Ginger's help, stagger over to the doctor who looked me up and down then referred to notes on me.

'Ah, young Gray, what have you been doing to yourself to get in such a state?'

'Circuit training sir,' I answered.

'What?' he seemed somewhat surprised by what I had said.

'You're grade two labour; you shouldn't be doing anything like that. I'll speak to Mr Hunt and sort this out, how are you feeling now?'

'Just a bit groggy, I should be all right in a while if I can go and lie down.'

After that incident I never saw the inside of the gym again and I did very little strenuous work on the earth shifting either.

+++++++++++++++

Benny King had worked his magic on the Governor and convinced him that it was essential to the running of the entertainments committee for me to have my guitar sent in as soon as possible. This entailed me sending in a written request, via the housemaster, to the governor for him to consider, then I would have to appear before him.

He praised me for getting involved with something worthwhile so soon after my arrival and granted my request. Moira brought my acoustic guitar up that very weekend when she came to visit and I set about getting my fingers back into trim again.

Some of the cynics in J2 came in to hear what I could do as they didn't believe that I could play at all. When they had all gathered around the end of my bed I whipped out a few blues licks mixed with some rock n' roll, which always sounds good. Then to clinch it all I did some finger picking that sounds clever but is in fact quite simple.

They went away grumbling and conceded that I could in fact play as well as I said I could but I felt that this wouldn't be the last I would hear on the subject. I made the mistake of telling them the names of some bands I had worked with before my present unfortunate situation; this would come and bite me on the arse in the future.

This meant that rehearsals for an impending show at the old folk's home next week could get seriously under way. It was the day before the tie board and once again the rules had to be bent to allow me to go. Receptions were usually not allowed to go outside the camp so special dispensation had to be granted for me. This was something else that seemed to seriously piss off some people in J2, who were already starting to take a disliking to me.

As there were so few of us on the committee the show would be fairly short. Kevin and I would handle the bulk of it by playing a lot of songs of varied styles. Brian and Andre would perform some comedy sketches, stolen from the likes of Morecombe and Wise, and a never-ending spiel of knock, knock jokes.

Still the old folks would like it.

+++++++++++++++

Time had rolled around at a pretty pedestrian pace; two weeks had now passed, not too fast and not too slow. The reception party had now come to an end it was time for us to be moved onto our various work parties. Tomorrow a new set of recepos would arrive, the discharge unit would empty out its occupants, taking their one-way tickets home then a new set would move in for their last two weeks.

I waited patiently as they read through the list of names on my party, most went on to the engineers or the farm party, and eventually my name was called.

'Gray, farm course.'

Round one to me, I was on the first step, hopefully, towards and early discharge.

* * * * *

Chapter Three
How They Gonna Keep 'Em Down On The Farm?

Once I had made my way over to join the rest of the farm party we were marched away from the parade ground and out past Jupiter house. The farm was situated on the outskirts of the Borstal grounds, near to the officers housing. It was made up of a number of buildings comprising the Farm Managers office at the entrance, next to the fattening house for the pigs, then the dairy.

Out the back was the swill hut where Kevin Ross would spend his time alone. Daily he would collect all the leftovers from the kitchen then haul them up by cart to the hut where he had a nice pot and stove to heat the swill up for the pigs. Over the coming months I would spend a number of hours in his little hut, keeping warm in the cold weather and talking music.

The two boys from the fattening house were Phil McGuiness and Tony Bates, a cheerful pair. Phil would become a very close friend and would save my hide on more than one occasion. I can tell you that he managed to keep my sanity over the coming months.

Next to the office was the mill, where Len Varley would mix the feed for the cows.

At the far end of the yard was the dairy where I was to spend the rest of my days at Gaynes Hall. In fact I can thank the dairy because I think I got out when I did due to my time there.

There were already three lads working on the dairy, number one dairyman was Steve Palmer. Steve was a bespectacled South African who had fallen foul of British law for some reason that never seemed quite clear to me. He held Britain in contempt, vowing to return to his beloved South Africa as soon as he was released. He did in fact do just as he promised as I received a postcard from Johannesburg not long after his release.

Steve held a lot of things in contempt, he was a very angry young man but we got on very well, despite his racial hatred. He would constantly refer to the 'kaffas' and how they would never be allowed to run South Africa; I often wonder how he took to Nelson Mandela.

He probably left the country.

Steve had some bushman skills, which amused a number of people, including the farm manager Mr Gibbons. He could trap and skin squirrels and rabbits; sometimes we would even cook the rabbits on Kevin's stove.

Sadly he hated the cows, and, if one of them displeased him, which could happen on a regular basis, he would beat them with a large lump of wood. I couldn't bear to watch it, and after once objecting to what he was doing I was told in no uncertain terms what *I* could do! Thankfully he didn't hold grudges when I disagreed with anything he said, he had his opinions and ways of doing things, the rest of us just had to accept them.

Gary Scott was his number two; they were like two peas in a pod, a real double act feeding each other the lines. They could be real fun to be around. Like a lot of the inmates of Gaynes Hall Gary had stolen one too many motorcars or TDA as it was known, Taking and Driving Away. Together they ran the dairy like clockwork.

Then there was Jeff Jones, or J.J as he preferred to be called, there is no other way to describe J.J other than that he was an arsehole of the highest order. For some reason he took an instant dislike to me. I think that he saw me as a threat to his position as there were normally only three on the dairy and my arrival upset the status quo. There would be a number of confrontations in the future, fists would fly and I would come to hate him as much as he hated me.

The most important person on the farm for me was Phil McGuiness, but more of him later.

The farm, although part of the Borstal, was run as a commercial concern. The milk from the small herd of cows went to the milk marketing board to end up on someone's cornflakes. Pigs were fattened up for market, as were the calves.

There were three civilians employed by the prison service, Mr Gibbons, the farm manager, was the boss, he was a very decent man who you could go to at any time with any problems.

Then there was the stockman, Paddy O'Reilly, if you try and imagine Claude Greengrass from Heartbeat then you'll get the picture, he dressed and looked just like him. Paddy, however, was your classic Irishman, ruddy faced and as strong as an ox as I would come find out. He could also be a bit of a crook himself!

Last, but by no means least, was Stan the farm hand, who was a real carrot cruncher! He had a very strong west-country accent, classic 'ooh arr, drink up they zider' if you know what I mean? He was there to assist us all in any way that we needed it; he knew everything there was to know about running a farm, probably more than Gibbons. His voice alone made me laugh, especially the way he said 'mangle wurzels', I'd been a fan of Adge Cutler since I was a schoolboy and Stan was a real Wurzel!

The dairy was our own little world where we were pretty much left to our own devices. It consisted of the milking room, where we could milk six cows at a time with the electronic milking machine. The cows would happily go inside, as there was a food hopper at the front where they could eat whilst being milked. Most of the time they were quite happy to go in there, especially if they were newly calved as their udders could be at bursting point.

Milking would take place twice a day, five o'clock in the morning and three in the afternoon. To begin with I was not allowed to take part in the morning milking, as I was still only a recepo. It wouldn't be until I became a TG, on my red tie, that I would be allowed to be at the morning session. Until then I would only be part of the afternoon session.

As it was winter the small herd, around thirty-five, were kept in the Dutch barn on the edge of the farmyard. Whilst they were being milked in the afternoon it was the job of J.J and ,me to lay a fresh bed of straw and fill the mangers with hay for them to eat on their return. A job neither of us particularly relished, and it was made no easier by having to do it together. J.J. would constantly attempt to Lord it over me, using his tenuous rank of number three to push me around. Initially I would bow to his superiority, being the new boy and somewhat unsure of my position. I have never been a fan of confrontation, especially when it seems, like in this particular instance, unnecessary.

I had only been there a few days and his aggression was getting more severe day by day. Eventually it blew up into a full-scale exchange of blows when he threw a shovel at me and demanded I cleared the yard of cow shit on my own. Steve and Gary had just left to take the herd back to the barn. It wasn't so much that the blade of the shovel had narrowly missed my head than I was sick to my stomach of his attitude generally. I picked up the shovel, now covered in cow shit, and threw it back at him.

'Shovel it up yourself arsehole!' I spat back at him, or something similar, I can't remember the exact words. 'I don't take orders from you.'

It slammed him fully in the chest, not hard enough to really hurt but enough to leave a large smattering of shit down the front of his overalls. That was it; he launched himself at me, grabbing my arm painfully whilst taking a swing with his free hand. At the same moment I pulled away from his grip with the result of his fist only glancing a blow to my forehead. Had it connected with the full force he had intended I would without a doubt have landed unconscious in even more shit on the cold wet concrete yard. Instead he lost his balance and it was J.J who landed in the aforementioned wet shit.

Unfortunately this did not improve his mood, whilst attempting to get up he swore that he would separate my head from my body. I believed not only that he meant to do just that, but that he was quite capable of doing it as well. I'd always been more a lover than a fighter but this was a new world where you couldn't just cross the street to avoid trouble. I knew that this was going to go very badly for me when the cavalry arrived in the shape of Phil McGuiness.

'J.J you obnoxious piece of shit, are you giving this recepo an unnecessarily hard time?'

'Keep out of this McGuiness; it's none of your business.'

Phil was a good head taller than J.J and in one smooth move grabbed hold of the front of his overalls and dragged him away from me to deposit him on his arse in a pile of cow shit.

'Well that's where you're wrong J.J, Kris here is my friend and you're not and I don't like you picking on my mate.' J.J sat unmoving in the wet shit, if looks could kill Phil and I would have been goners for sure. 'Now, I want you to treat my friend with the respect you expect him to treat you with, now do you think you can do that?'

J.J just glared back us both.

'I'll get you McGuiness, just you wait and see.'

'You've got me shitting my pants J.J, you're just a bag of wind, we all know you are so why don't you just get your arse off the floor and go clean yourself up before someone shovels you up with the rest of the shit. But, before you do that I suggest you help my friend here clean up this yard before Steve and Gary get back.'

I had to use all the control I could muster to stop myself from laughing, I knew that would not have helped the situation. I even held out my hand in a gesture of helping him back on his feet, predictably he declined. We both cleaned up the yard in silence, I knew that this would not be the end of it; I could feel the hatred coming from him every minute of every day.

With the milking over there was little else to do; the calves had been fed whilst the milking was taking place. The yard was clear now and the milking shed was being prepared for the morning shift, it wouldn't be long before the days work was over. I took a few moments to go and see Phil and bestow my heartfelt thanks for saving my arse. He and Tony were winding up for the day as well; as I poked my head around their door a smile came to his face.

'Still alive I see young cowboy.'

'Thanks to you,' I replied 'However, I don't think your friend and mine is going to let it rest do you?'

'Come in, you're always welcome here in the fattening shed, unlike Mister jerk-off Jones. I'm not worried about him and neither should you be, he's just a wanker full of hot air, stand up to him like you did today and he'll soon back off.'

'I hope you're right, it's bad enough being in here without having to deal with this kind of shit. Anyway, thanks again for you're timely intervention.' I put out my hand to receive a warm handshake in return, I had a friend in Phil McGuiness and that was something I would appreciate more than once over the next few months.

++++++++++++++++

Since strings had been pulled to have my guitar sent in before I became an STG, I had been working on my act, which was due to dazzle the old folks down at the local old folks home that coming Saturday night. Due to the fact that there was only the one guitar, mine, Kevin would need to use mine for his little set, no problem.

Every evening that week the entertainments committee had met to rehearse our show. With just a hand full of us most of it was resting on the shoulders of Kevin and me with such a shortage of other material. I didn't mind but I wasn't sure my choice of Beatles, Stones, Small Faces and Lennon material would be so popular with the over sixties set. Kevin would probably manage to woo them with his Latin American tunes and excerpts from the Leapy Lee songbook, for which he told me he used to play guitar. I think I would have kept that one quite.

I was quite looking forward to getting out that Saturday night, I know I hadn't been inside for long but it was already beginning to feel like a lifetime.

I had already made myself a little unpopular with some of the J2 inmates with my stories of bands and people that I knew. I thought a bit of name dropping might have given me some kind of standing in the community, I was out to impress.

I didn't realise how wrong I could be.

The day before the concert 'Machine Gun Woods' from J2, so named because he walked and talked like a gangster, invited me in to play a few songs for them. I knew I was walking into a trap but didn't have a great deal of choice in the matter. I was ushered into their dorm and manoeuvred to sit on one of the corner beds with my guitar whilst being surrounded by most of the members of the dorm.

'Come on then Penguin, give us a tune.'

'What do you want me to play?'

'Something by one of those bands you played in,' then they started to throw titles at me and began to laugh, I knew I had to get out of there and quick, so I stood up to leave.

'I don't need this bollocks.' I said as I made my way to the door.

'Just another bullshiter, like I said.' Woods said as I made my way, safely, out the door. However, that wasn't the last I would hear on the subject. A few days later I was pounced upon as I came out of the bathhouse. I was then dragged into J2 where a blanket was thrown over my head and they proceeded to beat me with boots held in their hands. It was over in a matter of minutes as I struggled out of the blanket and out of the door back to my own dorm.

If I'd learnt nothing else, I'd learnt how not to try and impress other Borstal boys!

Saturday night arrived and so did the minibus that would take the six lads, including my good self, and Benny King down to the village and the old folk's home.

Going back out the gate felt really good if not a little strange. It was only a short ride into the local town of St Neots where the small home sat in about two acres of grounds. We couldn't see much of the grounds in the dark and the rain but it was only a small place with about a couple of dozen residents. At one time it must have been a nice family home for someone with a bob or two. Now it had gone the same way as many similar places, either converted into flats or become one of the burgeoning army of old folk's homes.

Once inside they certainly made us feel welcome with cups of tea; sandwiches and cakes all laid out like a banquet for the Queen. Nobody mentioned what we had done to be in such a place and, thankful of that, none of us volunteered the information. As per normal there were more women than men, just like all our grandparents really, old, grey and slightly deaf, which was probably a good thing considering.

Thankfully it was warm inside; more than a little warm in fact as in no time I was sweating profusely. I know, as you get older the blood gets thinner and you feel the cold a lot more but this was almost tropical heat. I was looking around for the tomato plants, palm trees and coconuts but still the residents wore chunky jumpers and cardigans, just looking at them made me feel even hotter!

The boys went through their comedy routines, which brought some smiles to the faces of the old folks. Kevin drew a considerable amount of applause with his 'Girl from Ipanema' and a number of similar tunes. He was a natural with the old folks, he knew how to talk to them and put them at ease, I have to admit I was impressed.

Then after a few more comedy moments with other guys it was my turn to take the stage where I ran through 'Rocky Racoon' and 'Dear Prudence' by the Beatles, The Rolling Stones 'Get Offa My Cloud' and 'All or Nothing' from the Small Faces. I think they were pretty well received as was the all cast sing a long with 'Yellow Submarine' which all the residents joined in with.

After the show was over we had more tea and chatted with the residents for some time before we climbed back aboard the minibus, back to our cosy dorms and lights out at ten. I had a good evening and I think everyone else did as well. I was certainly looking forward to possibly going to do another one in the near future.

+++++++++++++++

One thing I wasn't short of in all the time I spent at Gaynes Hall was visits from Moira and my parents. For nearly every Sunday that I was there, one or the other came for the five-hour visit allowed. On the 21st of February, which was only two days before my first tie board, Moira came.

Unfortunately Mr Welch thought it would be a great wheeze to give me a love-bite the day before. Now try explaining that when you're in place totally devoid of females, not counting matron of course and the odd glimpse of Jim Hunt's rather attractive wife who wouldn't have given my neck a second glance.

We were chilling out on our beds after supper when he suddenly pounced on me with the help of Alan Mitchell, Gavin Coles and Steve Waller.

I didn't stand a chance. It was all done without malice but it left a huge mark that would take at least a week to go away and was impossible to cover up.

 Moira took it in her stride, at first concerned that they had intended to hurt me, but she brought her own tales of woe regarding Mrs Razzamatazz, who was attempting to sue us for a year's rent because Moira had left before the lease was up. She hadn't had any choice, as the rent was too much for her to raise on her own.

So now she had to move into a tiny bed sitting room in Queensgate West London, which wasn't helping with her mood one little bit. My parents were being very difficult as well, talking about my home leave, which still seemed a lifetime away to me. They were saying that I should go home to them but Moira wanted me to go to her, a preferable scenario for me as well, I don't think I could have handled my mother during that time. The atmosphere between them was stale to say the very least and something I felt powerless to resolve at that particular time.

During the visit we discussed the impending tie board. From what I could gather getting awarded the red tie was pretty much a foregone conclusion for everybody. That is unless someone had really blotted his copybook in the short time since arriving. I felt pretty confident that my copybook was squeaky clean and the tie was mine.

The day after Moira had been for a visit, a letter from her arrived, via one of the pirate mail services that were operating in the UK. It was thirty pages of A4; I would be surprised if anyone actually read any of it. Most of it consisted of what she was doing, finding a new job, a new flat and basically trying to come to terms with my not being there.

The tie board was a formal affair where we all waited to be called into the housemaster's office. For some it was a formality as they were not up for a tie but there were us few recepos hoping for that first one, the red. However there were a few waiting for green and a home-leave date or even more important, brown and the more important discharge date.

When I was finally called in, there was Bob Lewis and Ron Hawkes together with a member of the board of visitors. The board of visitors were made up of magistrates who in turn were ordinary people outside of the prison service. They would follow your progress through the Borstal system and together with the staff would decide on whether you would receive your tie or not. In this instance the visitor was a woman who gave me a blank stare as I came in.

'Hello young mister Gray' came the jovial voice of Bob Lewis 'and how are you settling down?'

'I'm doing all right sir.'

'Good well we've had some glowing reports from Mr Hunt on the reception party, pulled your weight and didn't cause any problems. Mr Gibbons from the farm has similar things to say about you so you will be pleased to know that you have been promoted to STG level and can go and exchange your blue tie for a red one tomorrow from the stores, take this with you.' With that he handed me a chit that meant I had the right to change my tie for a red one. Despite being more than a little confident that I would get it I was still elated as the words were still ringing in my ears as I left the office.

Everyone of my reception party was awarded their red tie, as was Russell Cohen, who had been demoted to a blue tie. He had recently absconded for the second time, hadn't got very far having been found trying to hitch a ride back to London on the A1, by a member of staff, Pratt. It was unusual for an absconder to be allowed back into Gaynes Hall, an open Borstal; normally they would be sent back to the Scrubs for re-allocation. This would almost certainly mean a closed establishment of some kind.

Somehow Russell had managed to escape this on both occasions, I never did find out how or why. Over the time I was in J1 six others went over the wall, one other came back but was transferred on the second attempt and another came back and stayed. I'll get to them eventually.

Other ties in J1 included a brown for dorm leader Pete and his deputy Phil and green for the two Chris's. There were a couple of disappointed faces, Kevin had hoped to get his three month green but everyone thought it was unlikely what with his obsession with an appeal.

I was happy; I found out later that both Moira and my parents had phoned to enquire about the outcome of the board. So they were happy as well.

+++++++++++++++

Having been promoted to TG, complete with tatty red tie, I was now entitled to a pay rise do the dizzy heights of 48 new pence a week! Britain having only just changed over to decimal currency one week earlier, there were now one hundred pennies to the pound instead of the old two hundred and forty. The ten-shilling note had already been substituted a few years before by the 50 new pence coin. The old two-shilling piece was now ten new pence and the old one-shilling was now five new pence, along side these old coins new ones were struck with the new face values. The old penny and half penny went and were replaced by the new half, one and two penny coins. The poor old half crown was consigned to history but the tanner, six old pennies stayed in circulation until 1980.

This change brought much confusion to a considerable number of the older members of the population and caused prices to increase due to unscrupulous shopkeepers. It ended over nine hundred years of the oddest currency system in the world. I didn't really care, it seemed a much better system to me as I wondered what to spend my first weeks 48 new pence on.

Back then I smoked and took sugar in my tea and coffee, both of these I have long since given up but back then drinks without sugar was disgusting. However sugar was a luxury not supplied by the prison service and if you wanted it, you had to buy it. There weren't a lot of items to spend your hard earned pittance on in the shop but sugar was one of them. I can't remember how much a bag cost but with my wages I could afford to buy a half ounce of tobacco, a box of matches (which with skill you could at least treble the amount of strikes), a packet of Rizlas (in plain packaging with HM Prisons printed on them) and the coveted two pound bag of sugar.

You could, if you felt really flushed, buy a packet of twenty 'straights', tailor made cigarettes, if I rightly remember only Players number 6 and Embassy were available. I rarely splashed out on such an extravagance. You had to be careful, as it was an offence to have more than one and a half times your week's salary on you at any time in either cash or goods. There were also a large selection of sweets and chocolate to be had, which I would eventually be able to afford.

Remember each Borstal Boy had to have ten shillings saved in his account before he could be sent on home leave. Matron was the banker for Jupiter house and I would put as much as I could in every week, sometimes bolstered by extra cash brought in on visits.

I would only stay at that level of pay for a few weeks until I joined the early morning shift at the dairy. We were allowed to work anything up to forty hours a week overtime at the princely sum of one penny an hour, riches the like of which I have not seen since! Mr Gibbons would always put the diary boys down for forty hours a week, every week, regardless of the number of hours overtime we did, sometimes it was more and sometime it was less. I couldn't tell you if I was ahead over the time I was there but with a regular income of almost ninety pence a week, I lived like a king.

One of the most sought after items was a two-ounce tobacco tin with a brass lid sporting your name. These were only available from someone who worked on the engineer's party. Pete James our illustrious dorm leader worked on the engineer's and we seemed to get on all right so when I asked him for one he readily agreed, all I had to do was get the tin. This wasn't a problem once I asked my father, he bought me a two-ounce tin of tobacco. At the time I couldn't have brought in that much so I had to take it in with just a small amount inside. I always thought it strange that we would be searched after a visit but not before so all one had to do was take an empty tobacco tin into the visit then leave with a full one, simple! Somehow I think they knew what we were doing but turned a blind eye to it.

As a recepo I was not allowed outside the dorm after work except to go to the bathhouse and then a TG or higher had to accompany you. There was a toilet in each dorm but the unwritten law was NO NUMBER TWO'S! If you wanted a dump then the bathhouse it had to be. Promotion allowed you a bit more freedom to move about the Jupiter house area, permission to leave that had to be obtained from a member of staff.

Promotion also meant that you could now be sent essential items and some luxuries. In my case the guitar, which the rules had been bent to accommodate, was already there. Now I could have shampoo, soap, toothpaste and shaving cream of a decent quality, unlike the standard prison issue that I had to suffer up until then.

But! The most important thing, after my guitar, to me was reading material. Each dorm had a daily paper, the Mirror if I rightly remember; which started with the dorm leader and finally ended up with me as the new arrival. What I craved were books and the music press, now I was permitted to have both sent in. So, every week from the beginning of March my parents sent me in the, sadly no longer published, Melody Maker.

It was the musician's bible, featuring a bulging small ads section where bands and musicians could look for work. In the past and in the future I would answer many of them, in fact it was because of an ad in the 'Smelly Melly', as it was affectionately known, that I left home at the tender age of seventeen, to join a band. It had first been published way back in 1926 until merging with the New Musical Express in 2000, a sad day. Over the next few months I would trawl through the small ads, mentally responding to many of them.

I needed to keep up with what was happening on the music scene, who was releasing new albums so that I could add them to my ever-growing list of what I had to buy on my release. The last albums I had bought had been John Lennon's first solo outing and the massive three-album set from George Harrison, 'All Things Must Pass'. Clive Dunn had been at number one with the cringe making 'Grandad' when I was first sent down but George had kicked him off with the hotly disputed 'My Sweet Lord' that stayed at the coveted number one spot for five weeks. He was sued for plagiarism by the publisher of the Chiffons hit 'He's So Fine'. The judge ruled that he was guilty of 'subconscious plagiarism' in 1981, some ten years later, when he would pay over half a million dollars in damages. Bizarrely, in a vain attempt to capitalise on the publicity, The Chiffons recorded a version of the song in 1976.

There were some great albums released in 1971 and I was eternally frustrated at being unable to rush down to my local record store to score my copy on day of release.

During my incarceration dad sent me a considerable number of books, mostly science fiction, for me to read. I left them all behind when I was discharged, donated to the library, accept for one. It was a book dad recommended, not fiction but about precognition and the human experience of time. It was by J.W Dunne and called 'An Experiment With Time', for some strange reason the officer on duty at the time it came in, can't remember who, took exception to it and refused to let me have the book.

Consequently it was put into my property for me to collect when I was released. For some reason I didn't challenge the decision and there it languished until my release date. I still have it and since then I've found a first edition hardback copy, but; almost forty years on I still haven't read it, I wonder why?

Further excitement came in the shape of 'the discharge suit'! For some reason, presumably known only to those in Whitehall, every Borstal boy was to be issued with a spanking new suit upon his release. So, as soon as you were promoted to your red tie you were to be measured up for it.

I was no exception.

So, on one wet afternoon the new TGS, all of us from the same reception party, were released from our toils to make our way to the library to meet up with the tailor. He was everything you would expect him to be, short, balding and distinctly Jewish. Standing with a waistcoat, a tape measure around his neck and a pair of glasses perched on the end of his somewhat bulbous nose. I guessed he was around forty years old, which to me at the time seemed totally ancient.

He was a fussy little Jewish man who would mutter to himself for a few seconds. Then he would stop still and poke his right index finger in his ear, cock his head, as if to think for a moment and continue what he was doing. Everyone in the library waiting to be measured up was desperately trying to stifle laughter as the strange little man shuffled around the room.

Before long it was my turn to be measured.

'And what is your name young Sir?'

'Gray, Kris Gray'

'Hmm....' He muttered to himself as he looked for my name on the list and I stood there like a lemon waiting for his next move. 'Fine, yes, ok,' he eventually found my name and pushed his bifocals up to the bridge of his nose. 'Please would you stand with your legs slightly apart?' I obliged, 'so Mr Gray what side do you dress?'

'I beg your pardon?' he heaved a great sigh to express his impatience.

'What side do you dress?' now raising his voice as if I would understand easier.

'I'm sorry but I have no idea what you are talking about, do you mean what side do I put my leg in first?' I could tell by the colour of his cheeks that my answer was not anything like what he meant. He looked around the room; nobody seemed in the slightest bit interested in what was transpiring between us.

'What side do your testicles hang?' he asked me through gritted teeth.

'I can't say I've noticed.' Came my reply, this instigated another heavy sigh from my new friend, 'is it important?'

'Not to me young man but it might be to you.'

'I can't imagine that I will wear it more than a couple of times so I think I'll put up with any discomfort I might experience!' with that he rolled his eyes around and aimed them at the sky before resuming his muttering to himself.

Having completed his intricate measurements he pulled out his swatch of the most boring materials I have ever had the misfortune to see. Not just the misfortune to see, as I had to choose which one my suit was to be made from and eventually I would have to wear the bloody awful thing. I've never been a suit person and other than this dreadful piece of sartorial elegance I have only ever owned one other, the one I wore for my first wedding.

But that's another story.

Whatever else I might have to say about my one and only encounter with a bona fide tailor at least it got me out of the rain for an afternoon. All I had to do now was get myself into the position of being able to wear it. However it would transpire that I would have to endure it more than once, besides discharge you were expected to wear it for home leave, something else I still had to look forward to.

There was one other time when I got to wear it, but again, more of that later.

+++++++++++++++

Meanwhile, back on the farm.

I continued to struggle with my tormentor, J.J. Granted we hadn't been physical since our Initial encounter when Phil McGuiness had stepped in to prevent my inflicting serious injury to the arsehole, well in my dreams that is. We continued to tip toe around each other, he would however, continue to needle me any time he could.

Phil McGuiness had become a good friend and we would visit each other on a regular basis. Jeff, I knew he preferred to be called J.J but just to wind him up I would call him Jeff or, if we were having a verbal confrontation, Jones, would not tackle Phil. Nor would he take on Gary or Steve so I suspect I became his whipping boy because he felt that he was theirs.

Now that I had been promoted to the dizzy heights of TG I was allowed to do the graveyard shift with the rest of them. I found this quite exciting; the night watchman would gently wake me at 4a.m, trying not to disturb the rest of the dorm. All the night watchmen were nice guys. They were civilian staff and not prison officers. One in particular, Reg, would have a cup of tea for me to drink whilst I got dressed. Then make my way in the dark to the farm where, together with Jones, I would bring the herd from the barn to the milking yard.

The dairy had its own kettle and an infinite supply of tea that Paddy would bring us; milk of course, was on tap. I would brew up as soon as the herd was safely in the yard and Gary and Steve had begun the milking. It was my job, which I didn't mind in the slightest.

Once I had finished drinking my cuppa it would then be my job to make the barn ready for the herds return. This entailed spreading a new layer of straw over the floor, covering all the mess they had left behind the previous day. The herd would spend all the winter in the barn; consequently the bed of straw would steadily grow higher by the day. Once summer arrived and the herd was put out to pasture, the farm party would then have the odious task of cleaning it out. There were many days when I would be thankful of being part of the farm course and not the farm party, the day they cleared the barn would be one of them.

My next job entailed filling the mangers with hay ready for the return of the herd. It was a bit like a carrot to a donkey, they knew that they would be fed whilst being milked with pellet shaped biscuits, then on their return to the barn there would be fresh hay. This helped to ensure that they would make their way there and back with no problems because, believe me, when a herd scatters it's bloody hard work getting them back again.

After a week or so of doing this task my hands were ripped to shreds. I had to lift the bales of hay by the string around them, cut it, then; shake into the manger; there was no gloves available to me. Not being one to complain it took a while for me to mention it to Paddy who had the solution for me in the milking house. Udder cream, udder cream is wonderful stuff; I wish I had some now. The cows would suffer from similar cuts, to their udders, for the uninformed that is the big sack thing that hangs underneath them and is full of milk. They would often be scratched by straw as well so we would apply this magical cream and once I used it on my poor damaged hands I was cured.

We never had any snow whilst I was there but plenty of mornings when the rain would be lashing down on me whilst I toiled at these tasks. J.J should have been grateful for my presence because had I not been there it would have been him getting pissed on and having his hands ripped to shreds.

While I was out there he would be in the calves shed feeding them. Once a cow had given birth the calf would be taken away from its mother, the bulls would be kept until ready to go to market where they would probably end up on someone's plate as veal. The heifers would usually stay to become part of the herd, having calves of their own one-day. So they had to be fed with powdered milk as what their mothers were producing for them would now belong to the Milk Marketing Board and one day end up on that same person's cornflakes!

Despite the continual antagonism from J.J, I began to settle in and quite enjoy the work. It wouldn't be long before Gary would be discharged then Steve would become number one, J.J number two and I would be number three. Not much of a promotion really as there were only supposed to be three in the dairy, all it really meant was that I would have a lot more to do.

+++++++++++++++

The endless Post Office strike finally came to an end on the 8th of March. They had been on strike for eight weeks, it had cost the average postal worker about £150 in lost earnings, that might not sound a lot in today's rates but then it would have been a considerable sum. The Post Office had also lost around twenty five million in revenue. It had all been a bit pointless really!

We had gone decimal during that time and the new first class rate was three new pence, an increase of two old pennies, just one of the many large increases decimalisation brought. Needless to say the Jupiter house office was deluged with requests for letters to write home. We were allocated two letters a week, post paid by HMG, which consisted of a single, lined, A5 sheet to get all your news on. I had still been getting letters from Moira via the pirate post; some were of considerable length whilst she told me her tales of woe.

At first Moira seriously considered moving back home with her mother. To be fair that was a non-starter, Moira and her mother didn't really see eye to eye and it wouldn't have lasted. Instead she had moved into a small room in Lancaster Gate but it was too far away from our friends. Most of them lived in the Earls Court area and she was hoping to be able to return there in the near future. It was possible that the house that I had once lived in was being partly refurbished and there would be something available soon. Moira was still in touch with the housekeeper, Mrs Hamilton, whom I had always been very friendly with, and she had promised she could have the first refusal on one. It didn't help my mood that I was unable to be there to sort all that kind of shit out, I don't suppose it helped her either!

Unfortunately it took too long for the work to be completed and she was unable to have the pick of the available rooms. However, a room at another house, only four doors away,where

Mrs Hamilton also kept house, became available. In the first week of March she was able to move into a fairly large double room in the same road I had once lived in.

So on the 15th March I sent my first letters home, one to my parents and one to Moira. I could now send her visiting orders, which I did with that first letter, and she came alone on the following weekend. It was good to see her without my parents being there, always good to see them of course but, well, it was better when they weren't there.

Over the next few months Moira would become friends with Russell's girlfriend, Tina, who lived in north London. She was a very pretty girl and I never fully understood what she saw in Russell. None of that mattered as the two girls got on very well and despite his stupidity, I got on with Russell. This made their journey on the train a bit easier to bear. There would be a bus from the station to Gaynes Hall that picked up all the visitors of that day, providing you were there at the right time.

+++++++++++++++++

Boredom can be a debilitating factor in most prisons; I was lucky to have plenty to keep me occupied. In fact I would say most of us in Gaynes Hall had a pretty busy life there. We were out at work most of the day and there were a number of evening events to keep you occupied if you wanted.

One weekly event, the dorm council meeting, was known as 'dorm agro'. This entailed our dorm officer, who in the case of J1 was Roy Hill, coming into talk with us after tea. I suppose he was somewhere in his mid thirties and connected with most of us pretty well. There was no set format to 'dorm agro', any subject was allowed, if the majority wanted to change the subject then changed it was. Roy was really just there to find out more about us, what made us tick and were we ready for release or should we stay, just a little bit longer.

We all knew what it was about but were happy to play the game. With no TV and only radio one to listen to in the evenings, any kind of entertainment was welcome. Roy could take a ribbing as well as he gave them, I remember him once saying to me that he thought I was less likely to be back inside, after being released, than most of others at Gaynes Hall. I knew he was right about one thing, I wouldn't be back but I couldn't speak for the rest of the lads.

Roy would sprawl out on one of the beds whilst the rest of us gathered around on the others. It was the only time that the no more than two on a bed rule was relaxed. We would discuss anything from politics and religion to music and any scandal that was occurring in Gaynes Hall at that particular moment.

Music was always a good one, especially with a couple of musicians amongst our number in Kevin and me. This would be even more interesting given the fact that he and I had such diverse tastes, as did everyone else in J1. The early seventies saw the emergence of the long, boring solo, which I have to admit, I thought was wonderful at the time. Especially if it was being played on a guitar and even more especially if that was by Jimmy Page, Jeff Beck, Miller Anderson, Eric Clapton or any of their contemporaries.

The singles chart in 1971 featured some pretty dire stuff, not much has changed there then. Sadly after five weeks at the number one spot Mungo Jerry and 'Baby Jump' evicted George Harrison. Over the next few months such dire 45's as Dawn's 'Knock Three Times' and Middle of the Road with 'Chirpy Chirpy Cheep Cheep' would occupy the coveted number one spot. Unfortunately I was unable to rush to the off switch every time one of these pieces of shit, and many others that failed to reach the top, came over the airwaves. The radio was controlled from the house office and you couldn't rush down there every time radio one played something you didn't like.

There was one particular session of 'Dorm Agro' when we managed to spend the entire period arguing over the difference between rock and rock and roll.

Alan Welch led that one; remember he was one of the biggest Hell's Angels from Croydon!

'You can't call this stuff rock music!' he indicated the front cover of my Melody Maker that featured a picture of Pete Townsend in full flight playing windmill guitar with the headline screaming out 'The Kings of Rock'.

'But Alan, that is rock music.' I countered.

'Nah, nah, Elvis is rock, Eddie Cochran is rock, Jerry Lee, you know what I mean?'

'No, no that's rock and roll.'

'What's the difference?'

'Well clearly there is one otherwise we would not be having this argument! Rock and roll is generally composed of a three chord, twelve bar progression.' I could see the puzzled look spread over his face, 'and rock music is far from that, often with chords that a lot of musicians have never heard of. So when The Who is referred to as a rock band that is because they know more than three chords!'

I think he grudgingly conceded to that one but he wouldn't admit to liking any 'Rock Bands', me, I liked both. Not a great fan of Elvis, accept the really early rock and roll stuff like 'That's All Right Mama', 'Blue Suede Shoes,' and 'Hound Dog'. Before Colonel Parker turned him into a 'schmaltz' singer and he made all those horrible films. The best career moved he made was dying!

One of the top stories of March 1971 was the final conviction of Charles Manson and three members of his so called 'hippy cult' for the murder of Sharon Tate. They were all sentenced to death; so, as you can imagine there was considerable amount of opinion to be had by all in J1. Surprisingly most considered the death penalty the right decision, that, Manson was so evil he shouldn't be allowed to live. Most of the dorm considered themselves to be 'honest' thieves, those who weren't protesting their innocence that is. So viewed murderers as a breed apart and should be dealt with in the most severe of ways.

Capital punishment is a very emotive subject and becomes more intense the closer you are to the subject. My stand is, and always has been that I am one hundred percent against it and I made my feelings felt.

'So what if someone was to kidnap your precious Moira then raped and killed her?' surprisingly Welch seemed very pro death penalty, 'I bet you wouldn't just 'turn the other cheek'?'

'I never said anything about turning the other cheek, sure I'd want justice but I consider execution to be legalised murder. Ok so this particular incident is a clear cut case, no doubt that they committed these heinous crimes, but what about the ones that aren't so clear cut?'

'If they've been found guilty where is the doubt?' a valid point from Alan Mitchell

'So where do you draw the line on doubt, if all the evidence points to a guilty verdict but the defendant still pleads his innocence, what then?'

'Hang the bastard!' was the rousing reply.

'But what if he *is* innocent, what *if* the evidence is wrong? If only innocent one person is executed, then that is one person too many.' I countered.

'Who was ever executed when they were innocent?' Welch pressed me.

'Well, off the top of my head there was Timothy Evans who was hung for the murder of his wife when in fact it was John Christie.'

'Who?'

'John Christie was a mass murderer of the sixties in Notting Hill Gate; he buried his victims under the floorboards and in the walls of his house. Timothy Evans and his wife were tenants in his house. Christie raped and murdered Evans's wife then Timothy, who, being a little backward, was forced to admit it by a corrupt policeman. I think you can be hip to that?'

With that there was a murmured nodding.

'Yeah but one isolated case.....'

'No, there are more. In the fifties, in your hometown of Croydon, Derek Bentley, again not the sharpest tool in the box, was in police custody when his mate shot a policeman. They had been trying to break into a warehouse but it all went wrong. His friend Christopher Craig had a gun that Bentley hadn't known about. The policeman died and because he was over eighteen and Craig wasn't, Bentley got the rope. How many others are there that we don't know about? And I'm sure there would have been a lot more had it not be abolished, at least there will be a chance of a reprieve if there is no death penalty.'

The point was conceded.

There would be many debates in 'dorm agro' over the months that I spent at Gaynes Hall, I wish I could remember them all, most of the time it was about nothing important but it gave us an opportunity to show the staff what we were all about. I don't think many of the others realised what was going on.

It was also possible to have a one to one with the one of the house officers by going into the office in the evening for 'a chat'. This was commonly known as 'grovelling', I would do this at any opportunity, it was part of the getting out early process, and I was determined to get out early.

++++++++++++++++

A month had come and gone, not swiftly I hasten to add, and the tie board was looming on the 23rd of March. In the meantime Harry Norton and Ken Smith had been discharged and we had two new recepos. One, Brian Kent, who would from that day forth, be known as 'Superman', I don't think I need to explain why, and Ray Collins. We didn't get much of a chance to get to know Ray as he absconded two weeks after he arrived.

Funnily enough it was on the night of 'dorm agro', he'd come back from the day's work, had his tea then disappeared. So absconding was the main subject that particular evening. Needless to say most of us still there thought it was a bad idea, especially Russell, who was the only one of us who had tried it twice and survived. I think most of us found it difficult to understand how he managed to stay at Gaynes Hall after the first attempt let alone the second.

Ray Collins was the first to 'go over the wall' whilst I was there, he wouldn't be the last, I'll talk about absconders further on.

I was only up for my first month on the red tie, just a formality really, but I was interested in hearing what they thought of me. I didn't have anything to worry about; when I was finally marched in front of the board they only had good words to say about me. There was the representative from the board of visitors with Ron Hawkes and Bob Lewis, who gave me his usual friendly smile as I came into the office.

'Ah young mister Gray, how is the farm treating you?'

'Fine Mr. Lewis, fine.'

'Good, well, again I get glowing reports about you, especially from Mr. Gibbons the farm manager; he tells me you are a natural with the cows.'

'Thank you sir,'

'Don't thank me, thank Mr. Gibbons, and see you next month.'

Of course I was pleased with my report and hoped that I could keep up the good work over the next two months as least, three months being the earliest time I could hope to get my green tie. Kevin received his green tie on a four-month red, for which he was extremely grateful, as did Chris Anderson and Chris Saunders.

At the end of the evening's excitement we all made our way over to supper for our tea and cake. Sure there were some happy faces but as ever some very unhappy faces.

Another month waited before me.

++++++++++++++

Since the guitar had arrived I had been feeling creative, being shut away was a frustration, I felt my career was slipping away from me. However, it was also inspiring me. Some of the dreams I was having were a little bizarre to say the least and not much has changed in forty years. It wasn't just music I was inspired to write but a book as well. All this occupied my mind and kept me from becoming too depressed by my situation. So I started writing songs for an album that would never be recorded. If I listened to them now I would dump most of them as some of the lyrics could bring back memories, not all of them bad.

As for the book, well, I have always been a science fiction fan, caught that bug from my father. So after having a dream about mechanical cows taking over the world I started writing about just that. The premise was that the planet had been invaded and all the survivors had a memory loss. The protagonist of the story, 'In Search of Myself' was I, written in the first person, the storyteller is searching for his wife, his only memory. I didn't finish writing it till long after I had been released, it was a load of old bollocks of course but had kept me occupied for a lot of the time that I had been there.

The more creative side were the songs. They were mainly based on the farm, my incarceration and Moira. Neil Young and John Lennon, my inspirations at the time, heavily influenced all of them. I bounced all my ideas off Phil McGuiness who was my muse, at no time did he ever tell me what I was doing was crap. What a friend, without a doubt a lot of it was undeniable rubbish, I still have the manuscript for 'In Search of Myself'. Publish it on my death if you want, literally over my dead body.

Rubbish or not, writing and cows kept me sane.

+++++++++++++++

Changes in J1 came about when Pete James was discharged. He'd been a great dorm leader who had been good to me when I arrived and I considered him to be a friend. He had a nice metal photo frame that he had made himself in the engineers show and donated to me when he was discharged, I never heard anything about him after he had left. I really hope he had a good life.

So the new dorm leader was Jim Groves, again a decent geezer with Ollie as his number two, again Ollie and I got on very well together. He was from the midlands, Sheffield I think, he wrote to me a couple of times after he was discharged but I never heard from him after that.

Come early April I was picked to be a sponsor for one of the first of the new intakes that month. He was a little Scottish guy by the name of Andrew Taylor, of course he swiftly became known simply as Jock Taylor. Like Welch had looked after me it was my job to show someone the ropes and make sure he didn't screw up in that first two weeks. Anything he might do wrong would reflect back on me, and that could have affected my record and subsequent release date. I decided not to tell him this as, not knowing what he was really like, he might have done things just to drop me in it.

Jock was from Glasgow with an accent so thick you could stand a spoon up in it. Moira was from the east coast of Scotland and her accent was a lot softer on the ear. Being used

104

to hers made my understanding of Jock's sounds of gargled concrete much easier to understand. I would very soon learn that small as he might be, someone to mess with he was not! He'd been very quite whilst settling in, like a lot of the inmates there he was convicted of 'taking and driving away' commonly know as TDA, or car theft. Not once, of course but quite a few times, this was his first trip to Borstal but he had previously done spells in an approved school.

One suppertime, thankfully after I had discharged my role as sponsor, he and I were sitting having tea and cake with the two Alan's, Welch and Mitchell. For some reason that evening Welch was doing his best to needle Jock who sat next to me but diagonally opposite Welch.

'So how do all you Jocks understand a fucking word any of you say?' Jock silently carried on drinking his tea. 'I suppose you're all used to it.'

'It's ney diff'rant t' ya sutern basdads, I kaney unerstant a wurd ye say eeder.'

'Woo ho, at least we're speaking the Queens English, Gawd bless 'er, what do you call that?'

'He's Queen yoos tarkin aboot, I have ney got ney Qween in Scotland, ya ken?'

'Ken?' Welch started to laugh 'who the fuck is Ken, the bloody King of Scotland or what?' he continued to laugh as he looked towards Mitchell and myself for support, he didn't get it, I thought he was being an arsehole and from the look on Mitchell's face, so did he.

'Wey d'ye ney ger oaf ma bark Welch?'

'Just wondered if all you haggis munchers talked the same and it's not just you who seems to talk out of his arse.'

I'm surprised I didn't see what happened next coming, it was all over in a flash. Jock leapt up from his seat, across me to plant a head butt squarely on Welch's face. He went down like a pack of cards to lay sprawled out on the dining room floor, blood pouring from his nose quite profusely. Just as quickly as he was out of it Jock was back in his seat as if nothing had happened.

Thankfully the duty officer was on the other side of the room and didn't see what had happened. Mitchell and I quickly helped Welch back into his chair, though he was barely conscious with blood all down his face and shirt.

'Shit Jock,' I snapped at him 'you could end up in the block for that, fighting is a no, no here, they don't like it, you could even get shipped back to the Scrubs for reallocation!' he didn't answer me, just carried on drinking his tea. Welch started to come to; we had to get him out without the duty officer seeing all the blood. Mitchell and I used our handkerchiefs to clean his face then pulled his jacket over the shirt to hide the stains.

'Do you think it's broken Al?' I asked 'Do we need to take you to matron?'

'Na, I don't think so, but it bloody well hurts.'

'How are we going to explain the blood on his shirt and our hankies?' Mitchell asked.

'He's going to have to fall over on the way back to the dorm, then we can get some first aid from the office, a clean shirt and some clean hankies. Alan isn't going to say it didn't happen that way, are you mate?' I answered with a knowing look at the injured party; he wasn't the sort of person to run to the office to say he'd been head butted by a recepo, which would not have done his reputation much good at all!

We waited until Welch felt strong enough to make his way out on his own. I told Jock to go back to the dorm while Mitchell and I took him into the house officer, who happened to be Bob Lewis on that particular evening. I knocked and entered the office with Alan's arm around my shoulder; he being bigger dragged me down a bit.

'Mr Lewis sir, Welch has had a bit of an accident on the way back.'

Bob Lewis looked down his nose at me, lifting one eyebrow as he titled his head to one side as he sized up the bloody shirt.

'Hmm, been fighting have we Gray?'

'Me Sir? Be serious' Lewis shifted the angle of his head from one side to the other as Mitchell shuffled into the room as well.

'Hmm, no somehow I don't see you fighting Gray, so was it you whose been fighting Mitchell?'

'No sir,' he replied, it was an accident sir, mopped up the blood with our hankies, look.' Showing both our blood soaked rags as Lewis's eyes narrowed, looking less than convinced.

'Yeah that's right Mr Lewis, I just tripped over my own feet, and lucky these two were there to pick me up again, felt right dizzy I did.' He sounded convincing to me and in the absence of any other evidence Lewis had no choice but to take our words for it.

'Then you better get him over to the matron's office to have him checked out, don't want any serious injuries now do we? You can take him on your own Gray, you can get clean handkerchiefs from the stores tomorrow, and a shirt for you as well I think Welch.'

'Yes sir, thank you sir.'

As we stumbled out of the office Mitchell shook his head and said.

'That was a close one, not totally sure he believed us.'

'No, I don't think he did,' I replied, 'but what could he do in the absence of contradictory evidence? Get yourself back and have a serious word with our Scottish friend on how we all have to live together in the same dorm.'

'Will do, see you later.'

By the time we got to the matron's office Alan had recovered his composure quite a bit and was able to spin the bullshit a bit better. I just grunted my agreement in the right places and she didn't seem any more convinced than Bob Lewis had been. She did manage to confirm that his nose wasn't actually broken, which was a bit of a relief. She cleaned him up, then gave him the customary two aspirins and sent him off to bed with the parting words that his face would turn all shades of black and blue by the morning.

She wasn't wrong.

Back at the dorm Jock sat quietly on his bed reading the newspaper. All eyes fell on the two of us as we walked back in the door; everyone leapt from their beds and rushed towards us.

'Is it broken?' was the primary question being asked.

'When you gonna kill Jock?' was another. Jim the dorm leader pushed his way through the crowd to look at the damage.

'Come and sit down,' he ordered Welch 'and Jock I want you to come here as well.' They went to Welch's bed where Alan sat and Jock, reluctantly, came over to sit opposite him. Everyone else, including me, crowded around as Jim sat next to Jock. 'Look Jock, I don't know what went down with you two and to be honest I don't really care, it's a racing bet that it was something stupid.'

'Ya man had bin pooshing 'n pooshing..' Jock sprang to his own defence, neither Mitchell nor I were going to do it.

'I said I don't care, what I do care about is that this dorm is squeaky clean, we're the best in Jupiter house and it's going to stay that way while I'm dorm leader, do I make myself clear?'

'Aye, ye de.'

'OK, good, now I want you two to kiss and make up, we all have to live together in here, bad enough being here without being at each other's throats, so shake and let's have no more of it.'

Jock and Welch looked at each other for a split second then looked away as they shook hands. With many slaps on the back from other dorm members the two protagonists gave a faint smile then Jock stood up to return to his bed and paper.

Believe it or not the two of them would become firm friends and the incident would not be mentioned again. In all the time I spent at Gaynes Hall there was often fights and bad blood between inmates, J.J and myself for instance, but all the members of J1 were tight. We didn't always like each other but we always supported each other.

Case in point, some time later we had a black guy come to J1, I think Jock was his sponsor but I can't be sure. His name was, and he always introduced himself as, Winston Everard Barrington Wilson, from the West Indies. In the early seventies you didn't see the amount of black people that you do today. This was before the gangs and what black people there were in England were basically hard working and good so it was rare to see one in prison and extremely rare at Gaynes Hall.

Winston was an ok guy who took everything in his stride and saw no bad in anyone, well not to start with he didn't. Sadly, that was soon knocked out of him, literally. He quickly earned the nickname of 'black enamel bastard', which he took in the spirit of humour though I'm not sure it was always meant that way. He was a big lad, who I am sure on a one to one basis, even two against one perhaps; he could have looked after himself, no problem.

However, certain members of the 'Devil's Dorm', J2, led by 'machine gun' Woods, seemed to object to his presence in Jupiter house, I doubt that things have changed that much. One day, when he was walking alone to the bath house, he was jumped by a large contingent of J2 members maybe even J3 and J4 as well, and was dragged in there. They beat him really badly and he was found semi conscious and bleeding profusely by a member of J4. He had a broken nose, a split lip, both his eyes were so puffed up he couldn't see out of them and he spent a week in hospital.

He told the housemaster that he didn't see his assailants as they had thrown a blanket over his head but you could tell from his injuries that no blanket had been used; just bare fists and other weapons of mass distortion.

But he told us who had been involved and we weren't having it, despite the fact that he could barely speak with the damage inflicted on his mouth.

At this time Alan Welch had become dorm leader and he gathered together Alan Mitchell, Jock and I with a few others to pay a friendly visit to our neighbours in J2. As protocol dictated, he knocked on their door and asked if we could come inside. Permission was duly granted and we all traipsed in to present ourselves to their dorm leader, whose name escapes me.

Welch drew himself up to his full height and spoke.

'What happened to Wilson is not acceptable and we will not tolerate anything like that happening again, to him or to any other member of J1. He might be a black enamel bastard, but, he's our black enamel bastard, so unless you want an all out war which will benefit none of us, leave him alone. Do I make myself clear?'

'Crystal.'

'Good, then I will bid you goodnight and welcome your visit to apologise to him when he comes back from the hospital.'

There were nods all round and we left. Needless to say the apology was never forthcoming but nor did Winston or any other member of J1 have any more trouble from J2.

+++++++++++++++++

Meanwhile, back on the farm.

I was still struggling with my nemesis Mr J. 'I'm so fucking cool it hurts' J. Given the right opportunity he would be doing his best to wind me up, to get me to make the first move towards a fight, an invitation I managed to resist for quite some time. The situation did not improve when Steve was discharged and everybody moved up a place. Gary became the number one dairy boy and J.J, of course, became number two. I came up from the lowly depths of dairy boy number four to the dizzy heights of dairy boy number three. My chores didn't change much; in fact they got to be more, as everything that J.J and I had done together, I now did alone.

It didn't actually bother me a great deal; in fact it meant I could be on my own without the mango chomping arsehole on my back all the time.

What it did mean however was that they brought me in on the diary boys little fiddle.

Now it doesn't sound like much but had we been caught at the time we would have been in deep shit. In fact it would probably have been seen as theft and our arses would not have touched the ground on our way back to the scrubs. Where we would have been moved on to somewhere nowhere near as palatial as Gaynes Hall!

We had milk, gallons of the stuff, in a huge container that resided in the next room to the milking shed. All the milk was cooled and at five in the morning, even before the milking started, there would have been enough to feed an army on cornflakes. I used to like to switch the motor off for a while, that would enable the cream to float to the top. Do you remember when you could buy cartons of 'Top of the Milk' before the days of low, low fat milk? I would skim the cream with my cup and drink it down with relish, if I did that now I'd be twice the size I am.

So, my new job as dairy boy number three; was to fill up four plastic gallon containers with milk and deliver them like the Unigate milkman to four of the Gaynes Hall officers. Who I am sure would have sprung to our defence had we been caught red, or in this case, white handed. I can't remember who they all were but two of them were Jupiter house's very own Jim Hunt and Kenny Forshaw!

Once I had filled the four containers I had to make my way out of the dairy yard, through a door between the milk storage tank room and the calves shed. Then, across a field to where the officers' housing estate stood, up into Jim Hunt's back garden to his shed where I would leave all four gallons of the white stuff. There I would find four empty ones ready for me to do the same thing again the next day; Christ knows what they did with so much of it.

For this little job we were paid the Kings ransom of half and ounce of tobacco a week, hey, you might laugh but when you have next to fuck all, an extra half-ounce was a fortune. So, this was another job to add to my morning list. It was ok in late March and April when it was still pitch black at five in the morning, but as it approached time to turn the clocks forward I was fast becoming a blot on the skyline. Now I was starting to feel more than a little conspicuous, and a little paranoid, as if a huge arrow was coming from the heavens to point out this Borstal boy on the fiddle.

I felt Hunt and his cronies' desire for gallons of milk shakes every day would see my discharge disappear into the dark, distant, dismal future. I wasn't having any more of it. So I pulled Gary to one side one day and explained my dilemma, he fully understood my point of view. Needless to say J.J didn't take it very well as he was making a bob or three out of selling cigarettes at half a new penny at a time, from his excess stock of tobacco.

We were together in the calving shed later in the day after I had delivered my bombshell. He was quite for a while but I could see he was boiling up for a confrontation.

'What's the matter Penguin lost your bottle?' I'd got used to the nickname, it could have been something a lot worse and anyway, it faded over the time I was there.

'Be my guest if you want to take over Jonesy, far be it from me to deprive you of your baroning income.

'Why you little shit!' he rounded on me, pointing the fork he'd been using to spread the straw around the pen we were working, in a very menacing way. 'You're just the shit shoveller around here, who the fuck do you think you are?'

For one minute I thought he was going to stick the fork in me, I have to admit my bowels started to feel a bit loose at the prospect.

'So what is it you intend to do about it? As I said I have no problem with you doing the job.'

'Yeah, but you'd still take your burn wouldn't you?'

'Well you've been taking yours while I risked my neck didn't you?'

'I was doing it before you.'

'But I wasn't getting a cut then was I?'

'Stop splitting hairs.'

'I'm not splitting hairs, it's true, now I want to get out of this place and if it means you can't get your half ounce of burn then tough shit. I am not going to put myself at risk anymore so get used to the idea!'

He huffed and puffed for a few seconds then turned aside.

'I'll get you for this one day Penguin you little shit, just you wait and see.'

'Maybe, Jonsey, maybe.'

'I will you little shit, and stop calling me Jonsey!'

I knew I had to watch my back all the more from then on

+++++++++++++++++

Easter had come around and most of the camp had a few days off, but not us poor lads on the farm. We did however receive a delivery of more than enough hot cross buns with lashings of butter. Together with gallons of tea to wash them down we had a fine day in the milking shed, milking cows, drinking tea and scoffing buns until they came out of our ears.

Moira didn't come to see me that weekend; she went to see her aunt Violet on Hayling Island instead. No problem, I knew I would get to see her the following week so my parents came instead. It was better that way as the trains were always a problem on bank holiday weekends so Moira had gone down to Vi's on the Thursday before Good Friday.

Dad however had to drive on the Easter Sunday, something I knew he would hate. When I was a kid and there was a bank holiday we never went anywhere. This was mainly due to the fact that he drove every day of the week in his job and wouldn't do it on a day off. The other reason he gave was that everyone else would be on the road going to Southend, the nearest seaside town, and he wasn't prepared to sit in traffic. At the time I felt angry and disappointed that we couldn't go but now, I sympathise.

It was always good to see ma and pa; mum would bring all kinds of goodies for me to eat. Cooked sausage sandwiches, pork pies, cakes amongst other extremely tasty morsels after which I would feel well and truly stuffed. This would mean that someone would have twos up on my evening meal, I'd collect it but it would get shared out amongst the lucky twos upper's. There would also be the much needed ounce of tobacco; again I would share this with the guys in J1.

This visit however brought some serious aggravation from them both. Over the past few months Moira had been making arrangements for our impending nuptials. This was something that I was looking forward to immensely, some light at the end of the dark tunnel that was doing time. Of course I was being blinded by loss of liberty and I am sure had I never been sent to prison I would never have married Moira. I was adamant that this was what I wanted to do, however it was something my parents more emphatically didn't want me to do. They had more than one very good reasons; number one, probably the most important one, was that I was far too young to even consider it. Number two; they quite rightly surmised that my being in prison was clouding my judgment. Number three; they just didn't seem to like Moira, who they thought was manipulating me and was partially to blame for my current predicament. There are many things I could accuse Moira of over the years but she was never to blame for my being in Gaynes Hall.

So, the majority of my Easter visit consisted of my arguing with my parents about Moira. Of course they were right about most of it, Moira was a bit of a control freak and I lost valuable time in my music career due to her, but that as they say, is another story. They were also right about my being too young, when I think back over it now I can't believe my stupidity, I blame the fact that I was locked away and it seemed like a good idea at the time something to look forward to.

I'll save all that for the next part of my biography, should I ever write it.

We didn't spend all that visit arguing about marriage and Moira; we also spoke about the slim possibility that I might be awarded my green tie and become a senior training grade, or STG as it was more commonly known. I hasten to point out that this was a very slim chance; most were granted STG status on the fourth or even fifth month. I didn't really think I was in with a chance but of course secretly hoped that I would get it.

Being awarded the green tie would mean being given a date for home leave. I could get out for five days, drink some beer, eat some decent food, smoke some more dope, and maybe even drop a tab of acid. I tried very hard to put that possibility to the back of my mind, expect nothing and you won't be disappointed, a motto I have tried to live by over all these years, and I have been disappointed, many times.

So visiting time eventually came to an end and my parents left with the parting shot of 'think about it son' which of course I did for a few seconds, then dismissed it.

Easter Monday was just like any other day, up early to milk the cows and a day in the dairy. This wasn't really a chore for me as it was extremely boring in the dorm with no much to do expect read, play Monopoly or listen to the radio and I didn't really fancy any of them so playing guitar to the cows was the order of the day.

++++++++++++++++

April 27th 1971 and the tie board had come around again, it was now my second month on the red. I knew there was no chance of getting promoted to green but it was interesting to know how I had been progressing. Kevin, who had already been on his home leave, was now on his second month as an STG. He'd got married during the home leave and was, naturally, hoping to get his discharge. I'm pleased to say that he did, he might not have had many friends in our dorm but, despite his tastes in music, I was one of them.

I had very quickly learnt that it was no good telling the officers what I really thought or intended to do upon release - this was a bad idea. At first I was telling them that I would be going back to re-launch my music career, bad move. At first I ignored their mumbles of discontent at my plans until someone gave me the heads up on what I should be telling them. Unbelievably it was one of the prison officers during one of our 'grovel' sessions, Len Forshaw.

We were discussing what I had done to be there and how I wanted to get back to my music when I was released. I had slipped into the office one evening just after someone else had slipped out. Everyone tried not to make it too obvious they were talking to an officer on a private one to one basis, it was basically frowned upon, hence the expression, 'grovelling'. I didn't really care and would make light of it if anyone made a comment.

'We'll see who gets out first!' I would quip, Len Forshaw was one of the easier members of staff to talk too and this evening was no exception

'What do you see yourself doing when you get out of here?' he asked me as he tipped back in his chair.

'I've always wanted a career as a musician so I'll probably look for a band to join.' He swung around about forty-five degrees in his chair whilst tapping his teeth with his pencil, not saying anything for what seemed like an eternity. I didn't know what else to say so I started letting my mouth run away with me. 'You know, write some songs, make a record, get a record deal, go on tour, probably in Europe as well as the UK.......' I trailed off because it appeared to me that he wasn't listening.

I was very passionate about what I was saying; I'd just turned seventeen when I left home for the life of a jobbing musician. My father had always been against my chosen path and it was the only way I could pursue it unopposed. I'll never forget the day I left, it had been snowing in early December 1969 and my father had slipped on the ice and broken his right arm. My mother was at work and I just left him on his own to cope until she came home, I didn't return until Christmas. I still feel guilty about that.

Eventually after a few more moments Forshaw stopped swivelling on the chair through forty-five degrees and turned back to the desk, folded his arms on it and leant forward in my direction.

'If you want to get out of here quickly, drop that idea like a ton of bricks.'

'Wha.........? What do you mean?'

'Look young Gray, Kris, I think I've got the measure of you. You've got a nice, very pretty, young lady who comes to visit you on a regular basis and your folks seem to be good people as well. I think you had a temporary lapse of common sense and I really don't believe you'll ever be back inside. Unlike a considerable number of your fellow inmates that I could mention, so I'm telling you this for your own good. Find something else to be passionate about before your misguided ambitions make a birdman out of you.' I was gob smacked! I didn't know what to say.

'Why are you telling me this?'

'Because I think you have already learnt your lesson and keeping you here any longer than needed would be counter productive.'

'Well I agree with you there.'

'And I like you.'

'That's nice to know Sir.' I answered, meaning it most sincerely folks! Len Forshaw, as I said before was one of the good guys, not that there was really any bad ones. Save for Jock the Block, a particularly nasty weasel of a Scotsman who was in charge of the block. The block was where anyone who committed an offence against the rules, for example, fighting, baroning, disobeying a direct order, and, absconding. If you absconded and were caught they generally brought you back to spend some time in the block before being sent back to the Scrubs for re-allocation. Jock the Block was the main man; still, once more I digress.

'Right now go away and think about what I said.' He paused for a couple of seconds then leant back in his chair once more. 'In the meantime, are you any good at making picture frames?'

'Picture frames?' I have to admit I was somewhat puzzled by his question.

'That's what I said, picture frames.'

'I thought that's what you said, well, er, as a matter of fact I am. My father is an artist and I used to help him make frames for his pictures.'

'I thought that was what he had told me, paints pictures and puts them in exhibitions.'

'That's right, he belongs to an art society, I used to go as well when I was living at home.'

'So how do you feel about making some frames for me?'

'Ah, yeah, sure, no problem' I knew that this would be an excellent grovel for me, a chance I couldn't pass up.

'I'll pay you of course, ounce of burn sound ok?' A chance to ingratiate myself and get paid for it as well, what a result!

'No problem, happy to be of assistance.'

'Tell me what you need and I'll get it for you.'

'A hammer, one inch pins, tape measure, tenon saw, a vice and a mitre block, enough framing wood to do the job and the pictures, best bring me the measure and the pictures first so I can work out how much wood you need.'

'All right I'll get them at the weekend.'

If I'd known then that my eagerness to ingratiate myself would almost get me, at the very least time in the block, I might have risked making myself unpopular by saying no.

However there was an even better up side to making picture frames for our Len. His wife, whose name escapes me but, let's calls her Sally, could not have been much older than me in her early twenties, she was very petite, no more than five foot nothing in her stockinged feet, with long blond hair. Oh and she was drop dead gorgeous, especially appealing to sex starved Borstal boys.

Sally would often cycle through the camp with her lovely hair flowing out behind her. We were especially lucky in J1 as the road from the entrance to the officer's housing estate ran past us and on up past the farm. This gave me a double chance to catch a brief glance of her loveliness as she wafted past, especially as the weather started to improve, 1971 having been a somewhat mild winter with a warm spring. She suddenly started wearing shorts while riding the bike and trust me; she had the shapeliest pair of legs that any man or Borstal boy could dream about having wrapped around him.

And this Borstal boy certainly dreamt about having those legs wrapping themselves around him.

This fantasy was made considerably worse when one day, once I had started my task, I encountered Sally on the road just outside the farm. It was quite late, maybe sometime after six. The milking had taken longer than normal and I was on my way back for tea. J.J had left a little bit before and I had stayed to finish cleaning the milking machine.

It was a nice day and I could see Sally cycling towards me complete with thigh hugging shorts, so tight you could see the shape of the lips of her fanny fighting to get out. How Len could allow her to ride around the camp like it I will never know. Maybe he got some kind of kick out knowing we were all beating the meat to thoughts of her in hot pants! Who knows?

As she got closer to me she slowed down until coming to a halt right by my side, stretching those amazing legs to tip toe to just about touch the ground. It took all of my willpower not stare directly at them and to keep my tongue from hanging out as far as it could go.

'You're Gray, erm, Kris aren't you?'

'Ah, yes Mrs Forshaw, that's right.' I was fighting to keep the tremble that was wracking my body, out of my voice.

'Len told me that you were framing those pictures for us.' She put her hand out on to my forearm, then, slowly slid it down to my hand. How I didn't cum in my pants there and then is still a mystery and a huge disappointment to me even now. 'Thank you so much, I can't wait to see the finished product.'

There is no doubt in my mind that she knew *exactly* what affect she was having on my libido. I'm sure the bulge that was straining to bust out of my trousers was evident at two hundred paces let alone up close and personal. Eventually, after what seemed like an eternity she finally let go.

'I er, I hope to finish them by the end of the week Mrs Forshaw.'

'Good, good, till then.' She gave me a last smile and a teasing look then cycled off into the distance leaving me wanting so much more. It was worth the trouble it almost got me into just for those few moments whilst she held my hand.

Sure enough, at the weekend, Len brought me the three pictures with a tape measure. I calculated how much wood he needed and he returned in the late afternoon, after my visit, with everything I needed. On Sunday I planned to make a start. It wasn't quite as easy as I didn't have a work bench to use, I knew I should have asked if I could have access to the engineers building but it was too late by this time. By the end of Sunday I had managed to cut all the timber to the correct lengths by clamping the vice to the chair in the cloakroom, it was my intention to put the pieces together over the next couple of days.

I had been working in the dorm's cloakroom, which is where I left the wood, but I put all the tools in my bedside cabinet for safe keeping.

I had intended to work on them during my hour off on Monday morning but I couldn't be bothered to be quite honest, I was too tired. So I left it, promising myself that I would do it after work, despite knowing I would be even more tired by then. My logic told me that I would have more time then, I almost had no time whatsoever!

It was just after lunch when Jim Knight suddenly appeared at the door of the milking shed.

'Gray!' I turned to look at him 'House Masters office now, on the double. Left! Left! Left!'

'What? Why?'

'Don't argue with me boy, get doubling away!' on the double meant you had to run-march, not too fast, not too slow but enough to allow the officer to keep up with you. My head was reeling, what had I done? I didn't have any contraband so what could it be?

It wasn't long before I found out as I was marched into Bob Lewis's office where laid out before him on the desk were all the tools. Every now and again the officers would conduct a search of all the lockers in the dormitories for contraband and any other item we shouldn't have, today they found my tools.

Relief flooded over me, I had an explanation and an officer to back me up.

'I trust you have an explanation for all these items that Mr Knight found in your locker Gray?'

'Yes Sir I do.' He looked at me a little unconvinced.

'Then perhaps you could share it with me?'

'I'm, I'm making some picture frames for Mr Forshaw and he gave me tools to do the job.'

'Mr Forshaw?'

'Yes, Mr Forshaw, Sir.'

'You do realise I just have to pick up the phone to ask Mr Forshaw if this is so?'

'Of course I do Sir, not much point in saying so if it wasn't true now would it Sir?'

'No Gray, I don't think you would be that stupid, however, I will speak to Mr Forshaw, you can depend upon that. In the meantime I will look after these and you can go back to work.'

'Yes Sir, of course Sir, back to work immediately Sir.' However I didn't move from the spot, still reeling from the shock of having been marched before the House Master on a very serious offence.

'Well get too it Gray, I'm sure you have work to do!'

'Yes Sir I do, right away Sir.'

I didn't need to be told again, I was out in seconds to make a very slow return to farm indeed. When I finally put my face back around the door of the milking shed, it was afternoon tea time and the farm party officer was having his afternoon cuppa with J.J whose face fell well below chin level to see me waltz back in.

'Thought I'd seen the last of you Penguin,' he scowled

'Well you haven't.' I snapped back.

'What was the problem?'

'No problem.'

'Then what was with the doubling away all about, you only get doubled away when you're in the shit?'

'Well, obviously I wasn't!' There was no way I was going to give him any information; it was none of his business anyway. 'It was a misunderstanding, that's all, everything is all right and I'm here to stay.' His forehead tightened as he narrowed his eyes at me, I could see the disappointment behind them, if he thought I was gone for good, no chance matey!

+++++++++++++++++

The Entertainments Committee was still something I was involved with, it had been a while since the Old Peoples home gig and now we were being called upon to entertain in the Officers Mess. I wasn't very keen at first, to be quite honest. I knew it would be seen as a good grovel and might earn all of us involved some Brownie points but I wasn't comfortable. However, on reflection, it was an evening I am really glad I didn't miss.

We were told to meet in the library after tea with whatever we needed to bring with us. There the steward of the club, whose name also escapes me, met us; well it was almost forty years ago. He took us along to the club that I hadn't seen since my recepo days when along with the rest of the gang I'd scrubbed their floor.

It was early so not many people had arrived, remember this was for officers and their wives and families; thankfully not too many children would be there. Not from my point of view but for the benefit of two of the officers present.

As a real treat we were allowed to have a couple of beers, in half pints I might add, but a couple of beers none the less. I thought I might save mine for after the show, it seemed like a good idea if we all did the same. Despite the fact that we were all gagging for a beer, we all agreed it would be worth the wait.

Eventually the officers together with wives in tow drifted in. All of us Borstal boys were all waiting patiently for the arrival of the delectable Mrs Forshaw. When she eventually made her appearance it had been well worth the wait. She was wearing a skimpy mini dress with plunging neckline and high heels. Inside my pants something became rock hard in less than a blink of my eye as it clocked the loveliness before me.

She knew what she was doing all right and on reflection I felt sorry for poor old Len as she swanned across the room drawing the eyes of every man and boy present, especially mine, and one other in particular.

More of that later.

Let the show begin! It would be nothing like the show we would see much later.

Andre and Brian did their usual comedy routines, which were well received by our captivated audience, or should that be our audience of captors? Kevin played his Latin American stuff on my guitar, I did a couple of Neil Young songs and felt brave enough to play some of my own compositions, which I'm pleased to say were well received.

Thankfully after an hour or so it was all over and we could sit in our corner where we could slowly sip and enjoy our two half pints.

However, the evenings entertainment was far from over, whereas us poor inmates were only allowed two half pints there was no such restriction on the officers present, and it would appear they liked a beer or two.

I didn't take a lot of notice of what was going on, a fair number of officers and wives came to speak to us poor inmates to thank us for the show and say how good we were. Always nice to hear, however I found it difficult to keep my eyes off the good Mrs Forshaw who seemed to be spending quite a bit of time with the cad like Mr Hunt.

It appeared to me that his attentions were just a tad more than a work colleague would make. So I turned my gaze towards Mr.Forshaw who was talking in blissful ignorance to someone else. Then I noticed another lady, sat on the other side of the room sipping a G and T who didn't look quite as happy, as her eyes appeared to bore into the back of the aforementioned Jim Hunt.

In the few seconds it took me to put two and two together and come up with the magic figure of four, she was across the room in a bound. She grabbed a hold of Hunt's shoulder to spin him round to face her.

'Do you two think I'm fucking stupid?' She screamed in his face 'do you think I don't know what's going on between you and this little tart?'

You could have heard a pin drop, even over the jukebox! Jim Hunt turned a brighter shade of red as his jaw bounced down to the floor and back again in the blink of an eye. My eyes spun quickly to Len on the other side of the room, initially shock had riveted him to the spot but in no time he sprinted over to hot spot.

'I……..We….. No, you…..' Jim tried to spit out a denial but a resounding thwack of his wife's palm as it slapped across his lying face silenced him. By this time Len was at his wife's side and glaring at both Jim, his wife and Mrs Hunt.

'What are you trying to say?'

'What is wrong with you Len? These two are shagging behind our backs, they think I don't know. If you don't then you're more stupid than I than I take you for.'

At that moment I realised that Len did know, or at least had suspicions that his little dolly bird wife was putting it about somewhere else. Perhaps he didn't know it was Jim Hunt but he knew it was someone. I felt so sorry for him; he was one of the good guys and didn't deserve to be shat upon by anyone, least of all his wife.

It was then that he took a swing at Jim Hunt who wasn't expecting it and his fist connected with the cheek just below his left eye. He staggered back with impact, over a table of drinks, to land with a crash of glasses and the dull thud of a head slamming into the floor.

Suddenly every man in the room was on the scene, holding Len back and tending to the extremely dazed Jim on the floor.

'Is this true? Is this true?' Len shouted at his wife

'Take it home Len,' someone said

The Governor appeared on the scene, he was quite an elderly man who moved slowly with a limp. He stepped in to the affray and immediately everyone backed off. He spoke quietly to Len who nodded, I couldn't hear a word, and then, he took his wife by the hand and left the room. Jim Hunt stood up, somewhat dazed; it had been a lucky punch I don't think Len would have got the better of Jim in a straight fight. I would have liked to be wrong. The Governor then turned to Jim and presumably had a very similar conversation as he also left, with his wife, within a few minutes

We Borstal boys sat somewhat dumfounded by the whole incident, not a word was spoken between us as the events unfolded. Within a few moments Bob Lewis sat down with us.

'I don't need to tell you lads that this **must not** go any further than this room. Should I hear anything from another boy all of you will be in serious shit, do I make myself clear?'

'Crystal Mr Lewis.' I managed to say after a few seconds, my mouth being somewhat dry, even after drinking my second half pint. "You can rely on us, can't he chaps?' I looked pleadingly at the others, not so much to save our skins but I didn't feel Len deserved to have his dirty laundry being made a subject of amusement around the camp. He deserved more respect than that!

'I do so hope I can young Gray, now cut along back to your dorms and let that be the end of the matter.'

Of course we couldn't stop talking about it as we made our way back to the camp but true to my word at least, the subject was never brought up again. Back at J1 Kevin and I were of course asked what it was like up at the mess. We told them about our beers, making all extremely envious but said other than that it wasn't much to write home about.

If only.......

I finished the picture frames and returned the tools to Len who gave me some tobacco as promised. Needless to say he had supported me over the tools incident and apologised for having put me in that situation. He compensated me for it with an extra ounce of tobacco. This, he assured me, had been declared to the office along with the ounce I earned for doing the frames in the first place.

I didn't say how sorry I was about his wife and the incident at the club but I think he would tell by my face and demeanour, how I felt.

Sadly, from my point of view, she stopped riding through the camp in next to nothing, in fact I rarely saw her at all after that. I don't know how things worked out between Len, Jim and the wives but can only guess that none of them stayed together for much longer.

Not my problem, I had enough of my own.

Because of my windfall it was party time and I made sure everyone in the dorm had extra to smoke for the next week, I was never going to smoke it all on my own. I haven't smoked for over thirty years and I didn't really smoke a lot then. I didn't need to sell tobacco; it would only have meant that I had far too much cash, so sharing in my fortune was the best way. Remember my parents brought me tobacco, which I always managed to smuggle in, it was easy to smuggle small items in.

Including some illicit substances, which I will come to later.

So, back to the April tie board.

I'd stopped talking about being a musician a week or so before but hadn't quite formulated what I was going to tell them instead. It wasn't a big problem; there were no complaints about my progress from the tie board.

There were some smiling faces as well as disappointments, Kevin didn't get his brown tie and Russell thought he might get his green having spent so long on his red but he didn't. There were a couple of discharges and another green, but to be honest I don't remember whom.

There were changes in J1, Jim Groves was discharged and we had a new dorm leader in Phil Johnson whom I became very good friends with. We met up once when I went on my home leave and swore to keep in touch, but sadly we never did. There were a couple of others who left us Harry Norton and Gavin Coles plus a couple of new arrivals. These included Winston, our black enamel bastard, and Phil Cramm who always surprised me that he had been sent to Gaynes Hall, he was so bloody stupid!

The new arrivals came because we had lost someone to the discharge unit. This had an upside for me, a proper bed with springs had become available and I was next in line for it. I'd spent two months on my extremely uncomfortable one with metal straps instead of springs. It was a blessed relief to find myself sleeping in comfort at last.

Another month had come and gone.

+++++++++++++++++

Meanwhile back on the farm.

Paddy O'Reilly, the stockman, was responsible for the well being of all the animals. He was the archetypal Irish farmer. As I said before if you think of Claude Greengrass in the early episodes of Heartbeat, you're close to what he was like. He was a big man, well over six foot, with a ruddy face, probably from too much Guinness or Jamesons, and as strong as an ox, as I would find out.

He had a small office just on the edge of the dairy buildings, but he was very rarely there, he was a law unto himself with no fixed times when he would be on the farm. Nobody could say where Paddy would be at any given time.

You could say he was a bit like the Scarlet Pimpernel, now you see him, now you don't.

Sometimes he would appear early in the morning during milking, often or not just to collect some milk for himself or to bring us our supply of tea. He was very rarely around when we did the milking, either in the morning or in the afternoon.

Paddy was an enigma.

He did however, know his animals, he would instinctively know when one of the herd or the pigs were unwell and the vet would be called. He was a good stockman; well in my limited experience of stockmen, he was good!

On a couple of occasions we had a major job to perform on the herd, giving them Iron injections. Now you would have thought that that would be an easy job but sometimes Paddy seemed to want to make it as hard as possible. We would bring the herd into the dairy yard then one by one take them into the milking traps where they were injected one at a time.

However, the younger cows, heifer's, that is cows that have not as yet given birth, would be dealt with in a different way. These would be brought one by one into a small pen, about five metres square. These poor animals were already scared and to be faced by the bulk of Paddy together with the trio of dairy boys was enough to frighten the shits out of them. Which invariably happened, they shat I mean, all over the place, sometimes all over us as we chased them around the aforementioned pen.

On one of these occasions, I can't remember why, we were one man short but we were so we had to recruit Tony from the pig house. He wasn't a great deal of use being quite a small lad so most of the time it was J.J and I chasing the poor heifers whilst Paddy stood swearing at us.

'Come on ye bunch of eedjets, catch the fookin beast, I want t' get back for ma tea!' commanded Paddy as he leant against the bars of the fence with a cigarette drooping from the corner of his mouth. With a bottle of iron solution in one hand and a syringe in the other waiting for us rustlers to bring down the steer.

They were all difficult to hold still long enough for Paddy to make the required jab. This time there was one who just seemed to have more will power to prevent us from succeeding than most of the others. I had eventually managed to get my arms around its neck but she was trying her level best to rid herself of me.

I held on for grim life!

J.J made limp attempts to grab a hold as well but I think he was enjoying my discomfort not to mention harbouring a secret hope that I might get seriously injured. Suddenly the young steer changed tactics and slammed me into the metal fence, which knocked the wind out me, forcing me to let go.

This brought even more expletives from Paddy but certainly no assistance.

As I lay gasping for breath in the straw and the shit J.J stepped up to the plate to have a go. He didn't really do a lot better and Paddy was beginning to lose his, laid back, Irish cool and slapped little Tony on the back, hard, sending him into the path of the charging heifer.

'Get the fook in 'dare help them get that fookin' beast down so's I can get this fookin' jollop into the fookin' so and so!'

Tony, of course, wasn't expecting to be catapulted into the ring with such force and stumbled as he flew into the path of the charging beast. He went down on the ground and the poor heifer's legs tangled around his body causing her to nose dive into the ground. J.J and I reacted immediately by pouncing on her in an attempt to pin the poor thing to the floor. It was working, but it wouldn't work for long, she was young and strong. Tony was pinned by his legs under her and was struggling to escape as Paddy advanced with the syringe out in front of him.

I'm not exactly sure what happened next; it was all a bit of a blur. Tony swore that Paddy did it deliberately; I had trouble believing he would do such a thing and J.J thought that he would but didn't think he did.

Somehow Paddy managed to inject half of the iron solution into the hapless Tony. What with his screams of pain and the frantic bucking on the heifer J.J and I were forced to release our grip on the poor animal and let it escape. Tony was also set free as it leapt off his legs and attempted to flee through the bars around the pen.

Paddy picked Tony up and slung him under one arm to carry him off to the hospital. He was a little under the weather for a few days but recovered never the less. Privately I agreed with Tony that Paddy meant to inject him, it made him feel better, but no one voiced that opinion to any other member of staff.

Paddy wasn't a bad man, he was just, well, Paddy, and Paddy was an enigma.

As I said before he knew his stuff, my first experience of birth was with Paddy.

Reg the night watchman woke me gently one night, about two in the morning to tell me that I was needed up on the farm. I shook myself awake, no luxury of a shower first in those days, and made my way in the dark to the farm. I was there before J.J but Paddy was waiting in the same pen where we had been injecting heifers with iron solution. In there was one of the pregnant heifers lying on the straw moaning quite loudly.

'Marnin' young Gray, I tink we have toime for a swift coppa before the main event, so go and put the kettle on will ya lad?'

So put the kettle on I did and was brewing the tea just in time for J.J to show his sorry face. He didn't look too happy about being dragged out of bed in the middle of the night.

'One of the beasts giving birth is it?' he scowled at me.

'Yes boyo one of da beasties are most definitely giving birth, as we speak, so down that tea and let's get weaving,''

I just about managed a couple of mouthfuls before going back out into the cold early morning air to where the poor young thing lay in obvious pain.

'Now der problem with this wee ting is dat it ain't not had a calf befores so the fanny is a little on the tight soide and it will be very hard for her to pop the babe owt.'

'So what do we do to help?' I asked

'Well Oim glad ye asked me dat young mister Gray coz you are going to assist the young lady. Now mister Jones here will lift her back legs apart.' J.J hesitated for a few seconds 'Come arn you eedjit we haven't time fer ya t' be squeamish, now grab the back legs and pull them apart.'

Reluctantly J.J obeyed, the poor heifers' moaning was beginning to get worse, like a woman, you can't tell a cow to push.

'Can ye see the tips of her hooves troing to poke dare way out of the fanny boyo?' Yes I could so I nodded my head. 'Good lad, now what Oi need you t' do is put ya hand insoide, grab a hold of them and pull 'em out as far as ye can. D'ya tink ye can do that?'

Well I didn't think I could do it actually, but I wasn't going to let J.J see that the idea made me shiver. So I rolled up the sleeves on my shirt and jacket and plunged in with my right hand first. It was wet and slimy, I'm not sure what I had expected but it was a most unpleasant feeling and it was not easy to get any kind of grip on the hooves, small as they were my hand kept slipping as I tried to pull them out.

'Come on boyo, Oi can't get moi big hands in there so you've got to do it soon uderwise she is going to have some serious problems.'

With renewed vigour I tried once more, this time I managed to do it, the hooves were completely out but that was as much as was going to at that moment. I sat back, sweating and gasping for breath, it had been very strenuous work. Paddy came over with a length of rope, which he tied around the hooves. Then went back to put her head in his lap and wrap his legs around the body.

'Now, you twos, grab a holda da rope and pulls wid all your might!'

So we pulled and we pulled, the calf just didn't seem to want to budge and the more we pulled the more pain the mother was in.

'Put ye hand back insoide and goide the head owt as well.' Paddy ordered, so I put my hand back in and I could feel the snout of the calf. But by doing that I couldn't pull on the rope as much as I had before and J.J started to mumble under his breath about it all being down to him.

Then, suddenly, as if she had been administered an enormous laxative, there was a loud slurping sound and the calf started to slide slowly out of its mother. In a matter of a few short moments the calf lay steaming in the straw whilst the mother panted with considerable relief and exhaustion. The placenta swiftly followed the birth; it was all a terrible mess but had been an absolutely amazing experience.

It had been my first birth, but by no means my last. I helped to deliver a few more calves before I left Gaynes Hall, but not all of them were that traumatic. On a couple of occasions when I went out into the field in the morning to bring the herd in for milking I would find a cow, waiting proudly with it's new born calf. It would be all cleaned and sitting with its mother; until we took it away. I always felt guilty, taking the calves away, never to see their mothers again, it seems cruel somehow. So we started to clean up this little tyke until the mother took over, we left them together for the rest of the night.

It wasn't worth going back to bed so J.J and I brought the herd in and made a start on the morning milking. It had been a tremendous experience helping with the birth of a new life and it was all I could talk about back in the dorm. However, nobody else seemed to be remotely interested in what I was telling them, except Russell who always seemed interested in what most people had to say.

Sadly the calf, which was named Ivy 2, died a few days later. It was the only calf born at Gaynes Hall whilst I was there to die and, probably due to my involvement in her birth, it upset me considerably

++++++++++++++

Paddy's eccentricity didn't stop at injecting Borstal Boys with Iron solution or generally being an enigma. He wasn't averse to a little pig rustling either! I'm afraid I don't know the full story but one weekend a lorry arrived at the farm and took a number of the piglets away. I was busy with the milking at the time and although aware of what was going on, wasn't directly involved in what happened.

There weren't many missing, about a dozen but on the Monday morning Mr Gibbons was on the warpath. He came in to the dairy to ask us if we saw anything at all of what went on. In particular had we seen a certain Irish lad from the engineers who shouldn't have been on the farm. Sensing that something was not quite right we all played dumb but I had definitely seen young Paddy, as he was referred to, as well as Paddy O'Reilly on the farm at the time.

I don't know how or why but young Paddy took the blame for what had transpired and had the bums rush back to The Scrubs and was never seen or heard of again. Rumour had it that O'Reilly and young Paddy had cooked up a scheme to sell the piglets to someone young Paddy knew. O'Reilly was reprimanded but due to him being virtually indispensible to the farm, managed to keep his job.

I don't know how true that was, prison gossip can be very vague and misleading, but the fact that young Paddy was shipped out seemed to substantiate some of what was being said. O'Reilly lost a fair bit of respect from the farm course boys over that incident. If we were wrong to suspect it was really all his fault he did nothing to change our opinions. I don't expect he really cared what our opinions were but perhaps he should have cared about our loss of respect for him.

That wasn't the last time O'Reilly involved the farm lads in one of his nefarious schemes. Again, on a weekend, he came to round me up along with Phil McGuiness, J.J and Len from the Mill.

'Oi've got a wee job fer yers all.'

We should have smelt a rat then because before we knew it we were all facing ship out to The Scrubs just like the poor hapless young Paddy. He took us around to the back of the barn where a trailer stood; normally we would use this to move hay or straw as and when it was needed. Today Paddy had something else to move and it had nothing to do with the farm.

On the weekends, other than the farm course boys like us in the dairy and the pig boys, there wasn't much sign of life around the technical buildings like the brickie's course, motor mechs' and the engineers. So when Paddy started to direct us towards this part of the camp we started to get quite worried about what he was intending to do.

'Mr O'Reilly,' I eventually stuck my neck out to ask 'what exactly are we going to do?'

'You's'll see soon enoof.' Was the answer I received, we all looked at each other with more than a little concern.

'But it's not something we could get into trouble for?' Phil asked as a back up to my question.

'D'ya tink I'sd get ye inter trouble laddie?' Phil didn't answer him, which spoke volumes and we were all thinking the same thing.

'Yes you stupid Irish bastard that is exactly what we think!' is what was probably going through all our minds but didn't quite have the bottle to say. Cautious looks passed between us all as Paddy continued to stride away towards the technical buildings.

'I've got a bad feeling about this, guys.' Phil was just voicing what we were all thinking, 'if we're not careful we'll be joining young Paddy back at the Scrubs!'

'There was only one of young Paddy,' I answered, 'he didn't have anyone to back him up, we've got all of us.'

'Look Kris, you know how it works, we're just convicted Borstal boys, no one is going to take the word of a Borstal boy, four Borstal boys or one fucking hundred Borstal boys. If we get caught doing something, even with the assistance of a member of staff we will get shafted well and truly no matter what we plead!'

I couldn't really argue with that!

So we continued to trudge along behind Paddy dragging the cart on a mission that we had no idea of what the outcome would be. In no time we arrived at the back door of the engineers for which Paddy seemed to miraculously have a key, we didn't question it, just followed him inside.

I don't know about anyone else but I was shitting myself.

Inside were some chairs, tables and wardrobes; all stacked up in the corner which Paddy made an instant beeline for. I could feel my stomach sinking very rapidly; it didn't take much imagination to deduce what he expected of us.

'OK lads, let's get dis stof ootzide and onta da wagon.' We all looked at each other with that same 'oh ma gosh!' look, Phil was the bravest of us to speak up.

'Is this all right Mr O'Reilly? I mean are we allowed to take this stuff?'

'Jazus McGuiness, what d'ya tink I'm doin' stealin' it?'

Phil didn't answer, what could he say? 'Oh yes sir I think you're nicking the stuff and I think we will all be in the shit over it!' I expect everyone was as nervous as I was but what could we do? What we should have done was walked away and let him get on with it, what could he have done? Said that we had disobeyed a direct order to steal some furniture? Forty years later it sounds so easy. Had we stood up to him there was probably nothing he could do, but we were all scared, understandably.

So we carried everything that he wanted out and placed it on the cart, stacked way up high. I can't remember how much furniture there was but it was certainly quite a bit.

'Okay lads, let's get dis stoof back t' my house as quickly and quietly as we can shall we?'

No one was happy at all, quickly and quietly he said, that told me that what we were doing was not kosher. I could see this all ending up in disaster and four little Borstal boys getting a one-way ticket to Wormwood Scrubs and fuck knows where else.

The cart was now a lot heavier than it had been bringing it there, a lot bloody heavier and therefore a lot bloody harder to move, which meant it would take us longer to get it back to Paddy's house. Every step we took made me feel like I could fill my pants; my insides were doing somersaults so much I was sure it would all come out in no time.

'Quick lads, into the trees!' Paddy suddenly turned back towards us; we were on the road back towards the farm and to the left were some bushes and trees. Without thinking Phil at the front of the cart turned the wheels to the left and we careered at an alarming pace into the bushes. Crashing through with an unstoppable cargo of stolen goods, whipping branches back into our faces and lacerating our arms in our attempt to stop it. Until, finally, an unscheduled collision with a tree brought it to a halt. This caused one of the chairs perched on the top to fly off and smash to pieces on the same tree.

'That's it' I thought, 'we've made enough noise to bring every screw in the camp down on our necks.' A sideward glance at Phil told me that he was thinking exactly the same thing.

I had no idea what or why we were doing this diversion, until I saw the Chief Engineer striding down the road towards us.

'Quiet lads, let d'man go by.'

If we hadn't been sure before, we were now; Paddy was up to no good, what we had on the cart was not something we should have had. I could feel my stomach sinking even lower than it had ever been and my heart was pounding so much I thought it would burst out of my chest.

'Keep quiet lads, shhhhhhhhhhh!' We watched as the Chief strode past where we were hiding and off towards the main camp. 'Jazus, dat wus close' Paddy exclaimed with a nervous laugh, I wish I could have felt the same as he did but my insides were still churning and my heart was still thumping away nineteen to the dozen.

'So, Sir, we are up to no good?' This time is was J.J who voiced an opinion.

'Well, maybe jost a little.' Came Paddy's reply

'Fan-fucking-tastic!' J.J. chipped in

'Great, thanks.' Phil added 'So let's get this fucking stuff to your house so we can get the fuck back to what we should be doing!'

As we dragged the cart out from behind the bushes and back on the road there was some considerable mumbling amongst the four of us, and Paddy looked a little more than sheepish. We continued in silence until finally reaching his house where our contraband was unloaded without being detected by anyone, more by luck than judgement. Paddy promised us all some tobacco for what we had done for him that afternoon, which he paid up a few days later much to our surprise. The incident was never mentioned again and he continued to do what he did without involving any of us in his nefarious pastimes again.

As I said before, Paddy was an enigma.

+++++++++++++++++

Towards the end of April, and I can't remember for what reason, there was talk of me being moved from the dairy to the fattening house with the pigs. Much as I would have loved to get away from the ever-oppressive J.J I was enjoying working with the cows more than I had realised. Eventually Paddy and Gibson called me into the farm manager's office to discuss the matter.

'As you know,' Gibson started to say, 'Bates is being discharged soon and we need someone new to take his place and unless there is someone on the new intake that is suitable, we want it to be you.' He then sat back in his chair awaiting my response.

'Do I get any say in the matter?' I asked, he and Paddy exchanged looks.

'Well, of course I am interested in what you think about it.'

'If I have a choice I would rather stay with the dairy.' I replied.

'But I thought you might like to get away from Jones.' I smiled to myself, quite obviously the animosity between J.J and I was better known than I imagined.

'I don't have a problem with him, perhaps he has a problem with me but I don't want to leave the dairy because of him.' As I said that an idea popped into my head. 'I have actually been thinking about a career in dairy farming when I leave here and have been meaning to speak to you about it before now. So, now would seem a good time to talk about it, if that is ok with you I mean.'

Their faces were a picture; I had suddenly hit upon the alternative that Len Forshaw had talked about earlier, no music. Gibson and Paddy looked at each other and nodded.

'You want to work in farming?' Gibson asked with a hint of disbelief in his voice.

'Yes I think I do.' I replied 'I have been thinking about going to college to learn more about dairy farming, can you help me?'

'Well, yes, of course I can. I can give you some addresses of agricultural colleges that you can write to and obtain their prospectus.'

I was getting into the swing of things now.

'Really, that would be fantastic, thank you so much, when can you let me have them?' I could see that they were almost lost for words.

'I'll find you some addresses in the next few days. So if you are really so keen to work in dairy farming we had better keep you there. So we will find someone else to take Bates' place.'

I have to confess I was somewhat relieved, despite my conflict with J.J I was happy in the dairy and didn't welcome any kind of change. I certainly didn't fancy working with the pigs, although it would have been fun working with Phil but somehow I thought cows were more my thing. However, eventually I would get to work with Phil when he was transferred to the dairy at a later stage.

Thankfully now, at least, I had escaped being moved from the diary. True to his word Gibson brought me some addresses to write to and any colleges or job applications did not form part of your quota for letters. I could write to as many as I wanted and still be able to write to Moira and my parents. He also brought me a copy of 'Farmers Weekly' for me to read, although not quite as engaging a read as the Melody Maker. Along with the Smelly Melly my parents sent me the FM as well, it was good to keep up appearances.

I'm not sure if all the officers bought into my new direction but the only one who said anything to me was the cad himself, Jim Hunt. During one of our 'grovel sessions' he voiced his scepticism of my new found interest.

'So you're going to be a farmer, are you Gray?'

'Yeah, I really enjoy working on the dairy.' He looked down his nose at me as if to say 'yeah, right!'

'Sorry, I just don't see you being on the job one night, down to the short strokes and some farm hand comes knocking at your door asking you to get up because some cow is giving birth!' I have to say I could only but agree with him, privately I couldn't see me doing that either but I had to keep the front up.

'Well it's not likely to happen every night is it Sir?'

'Maybe not but I still think this sudden interest in farming is all a put up job to get your discharge.' Without a doubt he had me well sussed but I couldn't admit to it could I? 'Having said that I will also say that I really don't believe you will step out of line again, I can't see you going back to prison, this isn't you, I don't think you're going to be a career criminal.' He was right there 'so I'll back you at the tie board, just don't let me down.'

'I won't Mr Hunt, trust me I won't'

And I meant it.

+++++++++++++++

At the end of April the engineers, complete with ladders and dustsheet, moved into Jupiter house to redecorate all the dorms. In all it would take two weeks and cause a considerable amount of disruption. They started with us in J1, which entailed all the residents moving out for a few days into J2, 3 and 4. I went into J4, thankfully, there were still a few unsavoury characters in J2 who I didn't really want to bunk down with.

It was quite crowded but a little bit of fun as well, especially with the boat vote as those of us from J1 were thrown out by just about everyone from J4, I would have expected nothing less.

Saturday morning inspection was also very chaotic; there was very little bed-space due to the four extra beds in the dorm. I was lucky having to go to work on the farm thus avoiding the actual inspection. However, trying to get my kit and space ready was a nightmare. You could barely move in the dorm with all the bumpers working furiously to clean bed spaces and the centre isle. There wasn't enough room to move the beds to polish the space beneath. Tempers, understandably, became a little frayed to say the least. Thankfully the staff took our discomfort into consideration during the inspection.

I was glad to get back into J1 after a few days to the overpowering smell of fresh paint, magnolia, of course, but at least it was nice and clean. However four members of J2 moved in with us as well while the engineers moved on to spread the smell all over their dorm too. I wasn't happy with a couple of them but felt the safety of numbers from my fellows, J2 members weren't very popular with most of us. There were no problems with any of them, in fact the past animosity seemed to have been swept away. I never had any trouble from members of J2 after that; helped I expect from the discharge of some of the worst.

Over the next couple of weeks we had the other two dorms bunking down with us. Despite the chaos it made a refreshing change to the daily drudgery of being an inmate at Gaynes Hall.

The week after it was all over and the paint pots, ladders and dustsheets had moved on to pastures new in Neptune house there was a new intake of Borstal boys. This time Jock Taylor was the sponsor for the new boy in our dorm; I don't remember his name so I will call him Tony Chapman. He was a quiet chap, but then so was I when I first arrived; at least he wasn't trying to come on as the big 'I am'! Unfortunately none of us had the chance to find out what he was like as he went over the wall just over a week after he arrived.

Like most absconders he went in the middle of the night. Their thinking was that it would go unnoticed for long enough to allow them to make their escape. For some inexplicable reason they didn't think that the night watchman would notice that they had gone. I didn't hear him go and I didn't notice that he had when I got up in the morning to go to work. Reg woke me up as usual and broke the news to me that Chapman had indeed done a runner. He asked me if I had seen him go but I answered truthfully that I hadn't, mind you I wouldn't have said anything if I had.

We were all questioned the next day but I firmly believe that no one saw him go. Someone would have said something to someone but no one ever did.

The Gaynes Hall grapevine spread the word that he was picked up in the morning breaking into a farmhouse to find some food and shelter. We never saw him again, although he was brought back to spend two weeks in the block before being shipped back to the Scrubs for re-allocation.

Most absconders were re-allocated when they went over the wall, the most notable exception being Russell who, as I said before, went and came back twice, I never knew how he managed to escape being sent to a closed Borstal, if you will forgive the pun?

Chapman wasn't the last inmate to do a runner from J1 whilst I was there. There were six in all, the most infamous being Martin Weiss, who was a very strange dude indeed. We struck up a sort of friendship due to our similar tastes in music, the main one being our love of the music of The Doors.

My schoolmate Tom had turned me on to them, when they released their first album way back in whenever. Tom and I formed a band at school, him on bass with me on guitar and another from our class on drums. We even played a couple of Doors tracks, My Wild Love and Five to One.

Tom and I had gone to see them play at the Roundhouse in Camden in 1968, on a bill with the Jefferson Airplane. I was a great fan of the West Coast sound and to have both bands on one show was amazing. Tom had managed to get the tickets, in those days there were no telephone or on line booking services, you had to go to the venue. I think his father went all the way from Essex to North London to secure them for us, maybe he worked in town, I really can't remember.

The Roundhouse was an old engine shed where trains were turned around. It had been built in the mid 19th century but was in disuse by 1867 and was eventually closed before the Second World War. It then lay empty until 1964 when it re-opened as an arts venue where live music was an integral part of its programme. This included the very first Motorhead concert in 1975 amongst a host of others, including, Jimi Hendrix, David Bowie, Pink Floyd and Led Zeppelin. Unfortunately it closed in the mid 80's and again lay dormant until a multi-million facelift in 2008 returned it to its former glory.

Tom's parents were a lot more liberal than mine and didn't mind their 15 year old son going to what seemed like the ends of the earth in those days. Mine would have had heart failure so I had to tell them I was doing something else, can't remember what I told them but my deception was revealed before the end of the day.

Camden was a bus ride, a mainline train and two tubes away from where we lived. Getting there had been easy enough but we hadn't figured on getting back. The last mainline train back home, we discovered much to our horror, had gone a short time before our arrival back at Liverpool Street Station. We couldn't call Tom's father as they didn't have a telephone, there was only one solution, and I didn't relish it one bit I had to call mine. It was bad enough that I had lied about where I had been going that night but to drag Dad all the way across to Liverpool Street to pick us up made matters a lot worst.

I think I was grounded for the rest of my life.

Weiss was wide eyed with envy when I told him that I had seen this show, he had never seen the Doors live. Jim Morrison died on the 3rd of July in Paris, seemingly from heart failure, aged only 27.

Weiss was devastated.

I didn't realise how much he had been affected by Morrison's death. So much so that when I went on home leave, only a week after it happened, I sent a copy of the Melody Maker to him with Morrison on the front cover. I wrote an inscription on the front to Weiss and signed it from Jim Morrison. I can't remember exactly what I wrote but it must have rattled him.

Weiss was a bit of an acid victim, I could see that and I think had he stayed long enough in Gaynes Hall someone else would have noticed as well. Although it was probably the best Borstal for him, what he really needed was some serious psychiatric help. I really hope he managed to get that eventually.

Somehow Martin had managed to smuggle some acid tabs through every step of his encase ration. From his sentencing through to The Scrubs and finally to Gaynes Hall he managed get them past every search, I know they are small and I don't know how many he had but you would have thought having been convicted for dealing in LSD they would have checked him out a lot more thoroughly.

So while I was away on home leave and after receiving the copy of the 'smelly melly' I sent him he decided to drop some of it and do a runner. I doubt that he would have got very far, acid or no acid but he must have been on a real hum dinger of a trip. Instead of heading for home, he made a beeline for the nearby village of St Neots.

Under cover of the night he broke into the small village church where he proceeded to wreak havoc untold. He smashed his way through the pews before finding a fire extinguisher that he used to destroy the font. He then went on to ripping up the bibles, the hymn books and prayer books before building a bonfire with them on the middle of the altar. It was just beginning to roar big time when the police arrived, following a number of phone calls from local residents regarding a disturbance in the church.

He was clapped in irons and the fire brigade managed to arrive in time to put out the fire before the place burnt to the ground.

Weiss wasn't the last to try and escape before I left but he was certainly the most colourful. He probably went into Gaynes Hall history as a legend.

Jerry Brooks, who decided to make a break just after breakfast one day, was gone for just over an hour when they picked him up less than a mile away trying to hide in a ditch. He was lucky; they let him stay instead of being shipped back to the Scrubs for reallocation. Unfortunately he tried again about a month later; this time when they caught him he never came back. Neither did Tony Palmer, who had come in with Brooks, he had decided to go out with him on the second attempt as well.

Dave Evans, another acid casualty, came in about six weeks before I was released. He was a nice, quite guy who was also very into the same music as me. I heard from Alan Mitchell, after I'd been discharged, that Evans also decided to try and escape. He spent eight days on the run, afraid to go home in case the police were waiting for him there, which of course they would have been. So eventually he walked into a police station somewhere and gave himself up. I think because he did that he wasn't shipped back to The Scrubs to be sent somewhere harder.

That was just the absconders from J1, needless to say there were a great deal more from all over the camp but I've no idea who they were. Other than Brian Walton that is, it was unusual for someone not to return from home leave but Brian Walton did just that. He was a particularly unpleasant character from J2; perhaps all the crap characters were deliberately put into J2, because it certainly seemed like it. Although he didn't have a discharge date when he left for home leave he probably would have been given one at the next tie board. However for some reason, that we were never a party to, he decided to take off, he wasn't recaptured in my time there.

Absconding, believe it or not, was never on my mind. I had the perfect opportunity, I left my dorm every morning around 04.30, most days no member of staff would be at the dairy to see who did, or did not arrive for work. If they did I could have been in the fields or anywhere else. It was only Paddy who might show up anyway and it was rare for him to stay for very long.

The dairy lads were always late for breakfast and therefore not part of the morning role call, so I could have had a minimum four to eight hours' start before I was missed. Moira could have been waiting close by with a car and we could have been on a plane somewhere before anyone knew I was gone.

But then I would have still been looking over my shoulder for the rest of my life wouldn't I?

++++++++++++++++

Meanwhile, back on the farm.

The time had come for Gary to be discharged along with Bates from the pigs. This would mean J.J being made up to number one dairyman and I'd be made up to number two with, hopefully, a new number three. However, things didn't quite work out that way and I don't really know why Gibbons made the decision he did.

A week before he was due to leave Gary, J.J and I were called into Gibbons' office.

'I have decided to make some changes to the fattening house and the dairy when Scott here is discharged, in fact I am going to implement them from today.' I shot a sideways glance at J.J, I'm not sure which of us looked more concerned 'Jones will go into the fattening house whilst Gray here will assume the position of number one dairyman.'

'But sir!' J.J stammered 'Why?'

'I want to change things around; I want you to start in the fattening house tomorrow. There will be a new influx of lads next week when Scott goes, so there will be a new number three in the diary.'

'But sir I……….'

'My decision is final Jones! Gray you will need a new number two, any ideas?'

'Well, if I have a choice I'd take McGuiness sir.'

'Hmm that would leave me a man short in the fattening house, but then there will be new arrivals so McGuiness can show Jones the ropes for a week then change over to the dairy.'

'I'm not happy about this.' Whispered J.J

'It's not my job to make you happy Jones, now get back to work.' J.J's hooded eyes bore into me as we turned towards the door where I let him go first, I thought I might get a knife in my back if I exposed it to him. He stormed away from me back to the dairy but I knew what would happen when I caught up with him. As I walked back through the door he pounced on me grabbing the front of my overalls as he pinned me to the wall.

'You put him up to this didn't you? You little shit! What did you say to him?'

'Get your fucking hands off me arsehole!' I spat back in his face as I grabbed his wrists in attempt to rip them away from my overalls. His grip was too tight so I swung my right arm up to punch him in the left temple. Bad move, he smashed by head back against the wall and I almost lost consciousness before he punched me in the stomach and I went down like a pack of cards. I'm sure this would have been followed through with a kick, probably to my head, as I lay on the milking shed floor.

But!

Tarrah! Phil McGuiness came to the rescue once again with a punch to J.J's kidneys. I didn't really see what happened next as I drifted in an out of consciousness but it didn't end well for J.J. He had to work the rest of the week with Phil so that he could learn the ropes of the fattening house. That was the last serious encounter I had with J.J as he was given his discharge date at the next tie board. Something I doubt that he would have received had Gibbons witnessed the fight, it probably wouldn't have done Phil or I any good either.

So the following week Gary was discharged, I would miss him, he had been a great guy to work with. Phil came in to be my number two for a while but he would also get his discharge date at the next tie board. The day Gary left a new set of recepos arrived and we received a new face from the old reception party as the new number three, his name was Todd McKenzie and he would become a great asset to me.

Todd was a burglar from Clapham in South London, an area I knew very well. He'd been to approved school a couple of times and had now progressed to a Borstal sentence. But he had another talent, he could blow one of the finest blues harps I have ever heard. As soon as he was given his red tie he applied for a couple to be sent in and then we were cooking. I would bring the guitar to the milking sessions, more often than not; then Todd and I would play the blues while the cows were giving up their milk. I proved to Gibbons that not only did it keep them a lot calmer but they also started to yield more milk.

Another feather in my cap.

++++++++++++++++

Todd and I had another thing in common besides our love of blues music, we both liked to smoke cannabis. However this was of course a major problem as there were no known drug dealers in Gaynes Hall. Well, there might have been but I never heard of such a person. Still feeling somewhat fireproof I asked Moira to bring me some the next time she came to visit. It was so easy, there wasn't really any supervision of the visits and she could pass it to me with ease. We were always searched when the visit was over, not too intensely but I wasn't prepared to risk it. However a visit to the toilet, unbelievably, wasn't subject to a search and I met Todd there where I passed a small piece over to him.

After Moira had gone I had to go back to the farm for milking where I met Todd with the contraband. We rolled up a number and went out into the field together to fetch the herd. Before bringing them in we took a slow stroll around the field smoking the joint we had just rolled. Having not smoked any cannabis for some time it went straight to our heads; well it went to mine at least. We spent most of the milking session that afternoon playing blues and laughing. Oh how we laughed, it was a good job no officer came around that afternoon, I'm sure they would have sussed what we were doing, well maybe.

Paranoia is, after all, all in the mind.

I wasn't the first person to bring cannabis into Gaynes Hall, the week before I came in there had been a bizarre incident with a guy named Dave Courtney. I was told that he had been caught in the discharge unit smoking a joint the night before he was due to be released. This really happened as it was the talk of the borstal for weeks afterwards and probably became part of Gaynes Hall folklore.

It wasn't clear how long he had had the stuff or how he had gotten it into the place, probably the same way I did. Still, he was on his way out, free at last. He was immediately banged up in the block and shipped back to the Scrubs the next day. He was charged with possession of a controlled substance and sentenced to a further term in Borstal. I don't know what happened to him after that.

I know I had been stupid and taken a huge risk bringing some into Gaynes Hall but at least I never smoked any in the camp. All the joints Todd and I had were in the fields with no chance of us being caught smoking them as we could see anyone coming ages before they came anywhere near us.

There was one occasion when I was convinced we would be sussed. Todd had been out in the field collecting the herd and puffing on a nicely loaded spliff. After a slow amble back to the milking shed with them we were both pretty high and enjoying a beautiful sunny day. As we herded the cows into the yard I walked into the milking shed whistling a happy tune, don't know what tune but I felt happy. Standing inside was the farm party officer, Dave Dalby, having a cup of tea, not really a surprise as, whoever the officer was on duty, often came around to us for an afternoon cuppa.

My paranoia hit full tilt, I was so stoned that I was sure it was written all over my face. Whilst struggling to pull myself together Todd started to bring the first batch of cows in for milking.

'I thought I might like to hear you two play something for the milking today, are you going to?' Dalby smiled as he sipped on his tea. 'The farm party are busy shovelling shit so I'm ok for half an hour or so, what do you think?'

What I thought was 'please fuck off and leave me in peace'! However even if I had put that to him more politely I felt, in my paranoid frame of mind, that it would make him suspicious and I didn't want that either. So I told Todd to roll out the harp so that we could play some blues to sooth the savage beasts.

Once we got started, difficult at first due to my fingers not quite going where I wanted them, a groove was settled into. Todd and I took turns in keeping the rhythm while the other took a solo, always sounds great to you when you're stoned, not always so when listening. Still Dalby seemed to be enjoying what we were doing and my paranoia gradually lifted with his first round of applause. Phil didn't smoke so at least one of the dairy boys was on top of what they were doing.

Eventually Dalby finished his tea and announced that he was sorry but had to return to the farm party and see what they were doing. I could feel the relief lift from my shoulders as he waved his goodbyes whilst wafting out the door. Todd and I looked at each other and heaved a somewhat hefty sigh of relief.

'Fuck! That was probably one of the hardest half hours I have ever had the misfortune to endure.' Todd wheezed through gritted teeth.

'Yeah,' I replied 'we are going to have to be more careful in the future!'

'Do we have much left?'

'Yeah, enough for three or four like we just had.' He smiled at me.

'Here's till tomorrow then.'

'Rock on!' I answered whilst lifting my cup of tea to raise a toast to the idea.

Needless to say we finished off the small lump over the next few days without any further incident. I'd had my adventure and wasn't keen on repeating it, I certainly had no intention of ending up with another sentence like young Courtney had; still, it had been fun whilst it lasted.

Someone who had been in Neptune house at the same time as I had been at Gaynes Hall contacted me recently. He told me that he'd been working in the kitchens and they had also managed to smuggle in some cannabis. Seemingly, he didn't have the exact details; someone would leave the drugs in a ditch around the playing field during the night to be picked up at a later time.

He also told me that they had some sulphate and acid as well but I was unaware of it at the time. What went on in the other houses tended to be unknown to those of us in Jupiter house because we were out on our own on the other side of the camp. The kitchen lads had also started to grow some plants on the kitchen roof but they were still there when he was discharged so didn't know what happened to them.

One of the things he said that really surprised me was that someone in his dorm had managed to procure a syringe from the farm. They were used to inject both pigs and cows, remember the incident where we had to give the cows jabs of iron? He didn't know who had managed to get one but my suspicions lay with J.J who was also in Neptune house. Some heroin had been expected to arrive but, thankfully, it never did, it could have been a disaster if someone had been caught with that stuff!

It had been bad enough, for the paranoia that is, being stoned on cannabis but I could never have handled an acid trip. I had taken a lot of trips during the year before I came to Gaynes Hall and being around straight people was never to be recommended. The idea of tripping around a bunch of straight Borstal boys let alone prison officers was not something I considered to be conducive to a pleasant acid trip, Martin Weiss a case in point! So having had my little adventure, which satisfied my craving for something I used to smoke in copious amounts, I didn't ask Moira to bring me any more. A few short years later I gave up smoking cigarettes, when my son was born, I then found it very difficult smoke anything else so haven't had any now for over 30 years.

Who'd have thought it at the time?

+++++++++++++++++

It was now late May and I had been deprived of my liberty for just four months. Remember my sentence had been a minimum of six months to a maximum of two years and it already felt as if I had served it all. Time was dragging, not like these days when Christmas seems to come around every week, if not every day, Roy Wood! My original ambition to get out before the end of the year had been replaced by a nine month term but even that was looking even more daunting every day.

Almost half of the members of J1 who had been there when I arrived had been discharged and I was becoming one of the more senior members of the dorm.

May 25th was tie board day; of course there was a lot of speculation on who would get what tie. The main topic of speculation was whether Russell would finally get his green tie, he didn't. Phil Johnson our dorm leader however, was granted his brown tie and celebrations were had all round. I was both pleased and sad to see him go, we had become firm friends, I would miss him. My Dagenham comrade Steve Waller also had his discharge, again I was pleased for him.

There were more disappointments and more surprises whilst my nerves were being fried as I awaited my turn. Eventually it came and I marched into the housemaster's office once more to face staff members and the board of visitor's representative. This was the first time that I had been nervous, previous occasions had not been as important as this. The blue to red was really a formality and as for the first two months on the red, well I knew there was nothing to expect there.

But this time............

'Gray,' housemaster Ron Hawkes looked up from his notes. 'We have had good reports from the staff on the farm, it would seem that you are a diligent worker, also that you have an affinity with the animals in your care. In fact Mr Gibbons says that you are one of the best dairy boys he has ever had, and if you pursue this as a career, as you say you will, then he believes you will be a success.'

'Thank you sir.' My heart rose.

'Don't thank me yet, I haven't finished, I should point out that Mr Hunt doesn't believe you will take up farming!' my heart sank. 'However ,he does believe you are a reformed character, as do the majority of the staff you have spoken to. Therefore we are awarding you your STG and you will be going on home leave on the second date which is the 15th to the 20th of July. Well done!' My heart burst through my chest.

'Thank you sir!'

'That's ok now keep up the good work.'

When I broke the news to everyone in the dorm, I had some friendly ribbing from most of the guys about what a groveler I was. Russell was not amused, especially as he had been passed over once again. I did point out to him that he only had himself to blame, if he wouldn't play their game by their rules he would always end up loosing.

Both Moira and my parents telephoned to see what the result of the tie board was. I think, like myself, they secretly hoped that I would get the green tie but what a surprise it must have been to find out that I had it.

There would be another tie board before I left on my home leave, now what a result that would be to get my discharge date on a one month brown.

Yes what a result.

Another month had gone.

* * * * * * * * * *

Chapter Four
Green, Green, It's Green They Say

The euphoria of being awarded my green tie lasted a couple of days, I was also over the moon to learn that JJ had also been granted his discharge and would eventually be off my back for good. Sadly my friend and protector Phil McGuiness was also granted his discharge. Again I was glad for him but sad for myself, we had been close and he had saved my bacon on more than one occasion, something I would be eternally grateful for.

Meanwhile, back on the farm.

Home leave was the best part of seven weeks away, which seemed like an eternity, and there were still cows to feed and milk. There were also some heifers to inseminate for the first time to enable them to become mothers and therefore yield milk. These days, even back in the dark days of the early seventies, the idea of leaving cows in the field with a rampant bull were long gone. If you wanted an efficient milk herd then they had to be inseminated at the right time.

Paddy always knew the right time for any of the herd; heifers had to bear two calves before they were considered to be adult cows. So when the time was right someone would come from the AI (artificial insemination) bank to do the dastardly deed. I was present on a number of occasions when he would arrive with his very long hypodermic. His arm, with the tip of the hypo in his fingers, would disappear up to his shoulder to find the right spot. Then, if all went according to plan and quick squirt and the job was done.

If all went according to plan that is.

Most of the older cows, that previously had more than four or five calves, were little or even no trouble at all. However, I do remember one particular incident with a first time heifer that wasn't having any of it. This took place one Saturday morning, Paddy was conspicuous by his absence and I don't remember where Gibbons was, that left me in charge.

We had moved the candidate into one of the stables the day before so it was an easy matter to bring her into one of the stalls in the milking shed. The poor animal was nervous enough being taken there; the ideal place to complete the task, but as soon as the AI man lifted the tail to put his hand up her she freaked.

Trust me, cows have a kick that can kill or maim, when that back leg thrusts out you do not want to be in range. Unfortunately for the man with the long rubber glove he didn't see it coming and the full force connected with his thigh. Not once either, I think she caught him maybe three times but the hoof flew out a lot more than that before she stopped.

Mr AI was writhing on the floor in agony as the heifer kept head butting the gate until it crashed open and she headed for the tall timbers.

"FUCK!" both Phil and I shouted in unison as the terrified animal made its break for freedom. Thankfully the gate had been closed to the yard and she could get no further than that. However, calming the poor creature down enough to entice her back into the stall was another thing.

'Leave her to calm down a bit,' I said to Phil, 'while we go and see how Mr AI is.' Mr AI was not feeling too clever but nothing seemed to be broken, however there was no doubt that massive bruising the size of a planet would occur. I suggested we made some tea and give the heifer a chance to cool off. Mr AI wasn't having any of that; he wasn't going near that mad beast again, well not on that day anyway. Poor bugger could hardly walk after his encounter with the flying hoof. Thankfully the well-shod hoof had missed his wedding tackle or he might have been speaking in a higher voice as well.

He was long gone when Paddy arrived to see how everything had worked out. He laughed like a drain when I told him what had happened, I was somewhat relieved as I had been in charge of the day and expected to take the flack for it, I still expected Mr AI to complain but hey, it wasn't my fault.

However a week later a different Mr AI returned to the scene; Paddy was on site this time and together with his magic words and my guitar playing we managed to sooth the savage beast. OK she still didn't like it but this time it went off without a hitch much to the relief of all concerned. Of course artificial insemination is not an exact science, like any mating. It can often fail, necessitating the return of Mr AI Man, thankfully our heifer 'took' and our wounded inseminator had no need to face her again.

+++++++++++++++++

Sometime at the beginning of May there had been plans for a trip to Snowdonia for some kind of work camp. It would have meant being out for about five days and Ken Foreshaw had put my name forward. Twenty names had been suggested for the ten places available. I'd been to Snowdonia back in the days when I had been a boy scout so other than the fact I could have got away from Gaynes Hall for a few days I quite fancied the idea of going back there. So made this known to anyone who would listen, how I'd been before and really liked the area.

Sadly that didn't help, I wasn't chosen, I've no idea why but a couple of guys who had been on my reception party did go, lucky buggers. When they came back I got quite sick of hearing about how great it had been.

In a way it was a good job I didn't go. There were two cats that lived on the farm and one of them was heavily pregnant with kittens. I had become very fond of Huey and Dewy, which was the names I had given them, no one else had bothered. They came and went as they pleased; there was no regular food for them, no tins of Top Cat. However I would often blag something from the lads in the kitchen and always put out a saucer of cream skimmed from the top of the milk store. So I think they looked upon me as some kind of benefactor and would come straight up to me whenever they arrived in the milking shed.

It was during the week of the trip to Snowdonia that Dewy decided to drop her litter of four lovely little kittens. She'd made a nest in the calving shed, with a little bit of help from me but I thought it was a bit to damp in there for them. So, I spoke to Ron Hawkins to get permission to bring them into the cloakroom of our dorm for a while. Surprisingly he said yes so for a week or so the little bundles of fur living in a corner of J1's cloakroom. All the lads kept an eye on them whenever I wasn't there and would bring tit bits from their meals for Dewy to eat to help keep her strength up.

I grew really fond of one of the kittens and for a while considered asking if I could keep it and let Moira take the little one home with her. Of course this was a daft idea, she still had our cat in the one room with her, bringing another in would have been insane, common sense however, prevailed.

Huey, who was probably the father, disappeared for a while, maybe that's what cats do; I mean it's not as if the cat version of the CPA is likely to come after him for maintenance is it? However he eventually returned when Dewy came back to the farm and the kittens had started to stand on their own four shaky feet. Eventually the kittens went to live with various members of staff, I was pleased they had gone to good homes rather than becoming wild like their parents. All except one that is who died at only a few weeks old, I was more than a little upset.

++++++++++++++++

Whether the increase in the milk yield was down to the music we played during milking sessions or the fact that the herd was receiving better treatment with Phil, Tad and I. Whatever the reason Gibbons and Paddy were more than pleased, so it was suggested that we joined the Young Farmers Club in the village of St Neots. This didn't sound too bad an idea as it would necessitate trips out of the Borstal to the nearby village. I was up for that, anything that got me away from the place, even for a few hours, was ok by me.

All the lads on the farm course said they would like to do that, not surprising really, so on the first night we boarded the mini bus with Gibbons and Paddy to meet the local boys in the village hall. There were quite a few of them, dressed in shirt, tie and jacket whilst we wore our Sunday best prison garb. I think they were as wary of us as we were of them, maybe a bit more, I mean we were convicts weren't we? Gibbons introduced a couple of the farmers who ran the club then they went the rounds of the names for the lads.

By the time all the introductions had finished I had completely forgotten every one of them. It didn't matter really; we only went a few times after that, I don't think it really clicked with either side. However, they had laid on a nice spread of sandwiches, tea, coffee and orange squash so it would have been rude not to make some kind of effort, which we did. Thankfully they all managed to avoid asking 'That question', they'd probably been instructed not to, but you could tell that they were bursting to.

I could tell that they all came from well to do families and had been well educated, they had that 'accentless' accent, if you know what I mean. I doubted that any of them would see the inside of a cell, but you never know stranger things have happened.

I didn't mind the practical side of dairy farming, in fact I was quite enjoying it but talking about it was a considerable bore. Unfortunately these guys could talk and talk about farming; it was obviously a passion for them. The size of our herd was also a bit of an embarrassment, a couple of them had over five hundred heads. I did point out that to them that five hundred would have been a drop in the ocean to some Texan farmer who might have over five thousand cows to milk. I don't think that went down to well with the carrot crunchers.

Still, what did I care? I was out for the evening, the chicken and ham sandwiches were more than tasty and there was sugar for the tea, luxury. So I continued to make the effort to sound interested in what they had to say. There was even talk of us going to the Peterborough show in July, a whole day out, now I was up for that! We did however manage to become quite friendly with the young farmers from the village and they managed to soften to us when they realised we weren't all axe murderers. It was a good excuse to escape the confines of Gaynes Hall for a few hours. I was writing to farming colleges at this time for their prospectus so I would speak to the chinless wonders about which was the best. At this moment in time I was still seriously considering going to one of them and it gave me something to talk about.

The Young Farmers Club had one outing to the Artificial Insemination Centre. I can't actually remember where that was but again it was an escape from the normal life of Gaynes Hall. I had heard all about Ringwood Leader, who was the super stud bull and it was interesting to actually see him. He was massive; this bull had serviced hundreds of cows on many farms up and down the country. I think his sperm cost more than most of the other bulls but I was assured that it was worth every penny. I believe that he would produce fine offspring and if they were indeed cows then they would produce plenty of milk. Well, that was the theory anyway.

I don't know how many times we went to the YFC, not that many but it was an experience I'm glad I had. It did eventually help me to decide that I didn't really want a career in dairy farming, but I had to keep the front up.

++++++++++++++

Visits from both my parents and Moira were very regular; I think there was hardly a week went by when one of them did not come to visit. Five hours can be a very long time, when you are stuck in one room and unable to go out for a walk of any kind. I wasn't sure what was worse, seeing them for five hours or not seeing them at all. Once a month for each would have been better but at the time I couldn't tell them that. They wouldn't have understood, either ma and pa or, even less so, Moira. I did, however, enjoy the packed lunches they would bring, especially mum's cooked sausages.

I think Moira saw it as an escape from the confines of the one room that was her prison, as well as getting to see me. She would often travel up with Russell's girlfriend, Pip, who was a stunningly beautiful girl. I wondered what she saw in Russell who seemed to me to be a very self-centred person. Sometimes the four of us would be in one of the visiting rooms together and there would be a considerable amount of banter going on between us.

Then one time, in June I think, before I went on my home leave Pip came and you could tell that all was not right between them. I think she was unhappy that he was still there after so many months and I already had my home leave date. Couldn't he just knuckle down and do what everyone wanted him to do? Sadly that was not in Russell's make up. Sure I could be a rebel but I was a rebel with a cause and Russell was a rebel without one. There was something that wouldn't allow him to play the system; he just had to buck it. I tried to educate him but to no avail, he was going to do things his way no matter what the cost, and it cost him Pip.

She came a few more times but they grew few and far between. I know they were never reconciled as I bumped into him once in the mid seventies. He wasn't the first, or the last Borstal boy to have his love life overturned whilst being banged up. One of the lads I came in with, who worked on the farm as a tractor driver, had a wife and child and she went off with someone else whilst we were there. Needless to say he was devastated but there was no compassionate leave for anyone in his position, just get on with it. Although, having said that, matron was always a sympathetic ear. Often the probation service would get involved, especially in the case of a married inmate.

I expect it all seemed so tragic at the time and if I spoke to any of them now they would laugh it off. I was lucky, I had someone who stood by me and didn't stray anywhere else, at least, I never knew about it if she did. She did wait for me.

When ma and pa came we would invariably argue, well maybe argue is too strong a word, about the wedding plans. Now I had a home leave date Moira was stepping up things on the wedding front. She was convinced I would be home by October so began making plans for the 9th, the day after mum's birthday and actually John Lennon's thirty first. She wanted it all to be a grand event; her mother always said she wouldn't come if Moira's father was going to be there. This was a big deal breaker, Moira wanted him to be there big time and her mother didn't want it, even bigger time. I didn't know how this would pan out but, like most things, it sorted itself out by her father saying he couldn't make it.

Relief all round, I don't know why she wanted it so much, she'd barely seen him since she was three years old when her parents had split. Instead of her father giving her away, her mother's neighbour, (who would marry her eventually,) did the deed. Moira was dead set on this being a church event, despite the fact that I was a devout atheist. It didn't bother me really; if it made her happy who was I to make a fuss about something I didn't believe in?

So the church in Redcliff Gardens was booked for the ceremony and a hotel on Kensington High Street for the reception on the 9th of October 1971. I agreed to all this but wasn't sure if I would be there. I had my green tie and although I hoped that I would get the brown at the next tie board, I wasn't 100%. I needed to get that tie to be out for the end of August, if I didn't it could be well into September or even later. I couldn't bear to think about that scenario, I would get the tie, I kept telling myself, I bloody well would get it.

With these plans overtaking me ma and pa stepped up their assault, trying hard to make me see sense, as they put it. Give yourself some time to re-adjust when you are released; get a job, somewhere else to live other than one room. In hindsight all very sensible suggestions, but I wasn't being sensible was I? I was locked away with only my imagination to keep me sane and my imagination told me that this was what I wanted.

Hindsight is a wonderful thing, isn't it?

++++++++++++++++

Other than a few half pints in the officer's mess once when we did the show for them I hadn't had a drink, naturally, since

I'd been sent down. So one day Phil and I hatched a little plan to brew something of our own.

There was a vast abundance of rhubarb growing in the gardens so Phil said that a small quantity of it probably wouldn't be missed. I thought he was probably right if we took a bit here and there instead of all from one place. So one morning whilst Todd went to fetch the herd from the fields Phil and I looted the garden, bringing back arms full to the milking shed.

One of the lads in Phil's dorm worked with the engineers, so, for a cut of the final product he managed to procure us a primus stove, with a full gas bottle. With this set up in the calving shed out of sight from Paddy and Gibbons, very early in the morning we started to turn the rhubarb into liquid slosh. We could only really do it then because Paddy was likely to show up and he never really hung about so the operation was easily hidden.

The liquefying of the fruit took us a week or so, there was quite a bit of it by the time we had finished. We'd stored it all in one of the unused milk urns stored in the back of the calving shed. I think there must have been about five gallons of the stuff, what we need next was some yeast. So a visit to the boys in the kitchen, who made the bread for everyone, was in order, they were sure to have an abundance of the stuff.

The kitchen officer was also never around first thing in the morning. I had spoken to my mate Ian, who had been on the reception party with me. He promised me a few packets if I could get around to the kitchen before we went up to the farm one morning. Phil and I met up outside, we both needed to be there to distribute the packets between us. This was in case of the unlikely event of us bumping into an officer before getting back to the farm.

Phil was there on time. Our story, if there was an officer in situ, was that we had run out of tea and Paddy hadn't brought us any. However our fears were unnecessary as the bustling kitchen was devoid of any officers. It was hot inside, not that it was particularly cold outside, even at such an early hour in June. With all the ovens going full tilt baking bread the heat and pies for lunch was quite intense. Ian brought out four packets of yeast, Phil and I took two each and stowed them away in our dungarees. I thanked him and reassured the kitchen crew that they would all get some of our brew when it was ready. We turned to open the door but before either of us had a chance to put our hand on the handle it sprung open before us. There standing in the doorway was the head cook, not technically a prison office but like Gibbons, employed by the prison service.

'Hello,' he boomed 'Who do we have here?' Shit! I thought, if he searches us we are well and truly fucked, goodbye green tie and home leave for me and goodbye discharge for Phil.

'Morning Sir, I managed to say without too much of a wobble in my voice. 'We're Gray and McGuiness from the dairy.'

'Really?' he replied 'Unless I'm very much mistaken the dairy is up the other end of the camp.' I gave him a genial smile whilst trying to look normal, stick to the story we had planned I thought.

'They came for some tea Sir,' Ian chipped in quickly, great minds think alike.

'I thought Mr O'Reilly provided your tea?'

'That's what I said Sir, and I couldn't supply them without your say so.' Cookie looked at me then to Phil and back again.

'No loaves of bread tucked up your jumper then lads?' Phil started to laugh, I thought 'oh no don't laugh'

'I think you might just see a loaf of bread if it was bulging out of my jumper Sir.' Phil blurted out.

'I'm sure I would laddie,' he turned to Ian 'so give them enough for a morning cuppa, I'm sure Paddy will be around with your supply soon enough.'

'Thank you sir.' Was just about all Phil and I could manage whilst keeping a straight face as Ian gave us a bag of tea before hustling us out of the door.

'That was close!' he said as we slipped past him 'Let's not do this again eh?' I just grinned back at him as Phil and I made our escape complete with our ill gotten yeast.

Back at the farm we weren't really quite sure what to do with the yeast. I suggested we broke it up and put it in the urn with the liquefied fruit. With the absence of a better idea, that's exactly what we did laughing manaically at the same time. How long this was supposed to ferment, of course none of us had any idea. What we wanted to do was drink it the next day but of course even we knew that this wouldn't be possible. We hid the urn under a pile of straw in the corner of one of the pens in the calving shed, unlikely that anyone would stumble upon it there.

Sadly the anticipated rhubarb wine party was not to be. Having involved someone from the engineers and the entire kitchen staff, tongues had been wagging. When Alan Mitchell, who was on the motor mechanics course (remember?) asked me when the hooch was going to be ready, I knew we were in trouble. If he knew then it wouldn't be long before one of the officers got to hear about it. I wasn't going to take any chances so I called a hasty meeting of the Gaynes Hall Dairy Brewers Society.

I said that I thought too many people had gotten wind of what we were doing. As soon as I did both Phil and Todd said lads in their dorm had approached them for some of the brew. I was beside myself, why hadn't they mentioned it before? This was a serious situation that I wanted out of tout suite! Both of them assured me that they had sworn the others to total silence but knew this was too dangerous to continue.

So, the next morning whilst Phil and Todd were milking the herd I poured the entire contents of the urn down the drain that lived between the dairy yard and the road outside. It hurt to me do it as we had spent a lot of time and energy on it. A lot of risks had been taken by, not only us but also the engineers who had supplied the primus and the kitchen lads with the yeast.

The smell of alcohol as I poured the gallons away was overpowering. I'd picked the wrong place to do it, if Paddy had come through there at any time during that day he would have smelt it no problem.

When I look back on it I can see the funny side of what we had been trying to do. However, had we been caught at any time during the production of our rhubarb wine I'm sure that we would have been up to our necks in shit. Stealing from the gardens was bad enough, and then illegal use of a primus stove followed by theft of yeast from the kitchen. I'm sure Ian in the kitchen and the lad from the engineers would have felt the wrath of the system as well.

If they had wanted to, the powers that be could have brought criminal charges against us all. Loss of everything we had all been working for, getting out. It would have been bad enough for me to suffer for what few had done but for everyone else to suffer as well would have been more than I could have taken. I'm not sure if ma, pa and Moira would have ever forgiven me.

Thankfully it had never come to that, when I broke the news to Ian as to what I had done he understood, so did the lad on the engineers. The incident was never spoken about again.

+++++++++++++++

The Entertainments committee was still thriving well into June as all of us who had formed it way back in January were still at Gaynes Hall. Having said that Kevin was now in the discharge unit counting off the last few days to discharge and had very little interest in our exploits. However I had managed to rope Todd and his mean harp in to joining us so that we could play a little blues together. The committee had been invited by the village cricket club to come and entertain them on one Saturday night in June.

When we had completed the afternoon milking Todd and I went back to our respective dorms to scrub up and change into our best prison blues. Then armed with our respective instruments we met up with Bernie King and the minibus out of Dodge. We had been invited to play a short game with them before having tea and sarnies prior to the main event. Now the idea of playing cricket, probably the world's second most boring game, just behind golf, but only marginally, did not appeal to me one little bit.

Whilst being forced to endure the game when I was at school it was discovered that I had two left hands and was unable to catch a cricket ball. The idea of a large lump of wood and leather hurtling towards me at close to the speed of a bullet did not appeal. It also seemed that the only players getting any action were the bowler and the batsman. The rest of the team could snooze while waiting for the ball to come their way. I wasn't much better at football either where I discovered that I had two left feet. I was finally spared the indignity of being the last boy chosen for a class team when I contracted tuberculosis at the age of fourteen. I'll never forget the doctor's sombre words when he told me that I had TB.

'I'm sorry young man but you won't be able to play football for some time.'

'Fantastic!' was my reply, I don't think it was quite the response he was expecting.

So there we were on the village green, just like out of the Kinks song 'We Are the Village Green Preservation Society'. A lovely early summers evening with the team all decked out in their whites waiting for us. As we were introduced they made us all feel very welcome and not like a bunch of train robbers. They laid on some ice cold lemonade and ginger beer, which was gratefully accepted. The cricket team split to make two teams, as there were only four of us Borstal boys Todd and I went on one team whilst Brian and Andre joined the others. Before even one ball was bowled I felt very sorry for my team, there was very little chance that they could win with me on board.

I wasn't far wrong!

Due to time being short it was proposed that each team would play as the 'in' team for half an hour each then whoever had the most runs would be the winner. The other team won the toss and went in first. Being the gentlemen that they were they allowed our two lads to bat first, good move on their part and bad luck on ours. Brian turned out to be a magnificent batsman; I was, needless to say, a crap bowler who managed to deliver the balls just as he needed them. Even after my over he continued to send the balls far and wide. After their half an hour was up Brian was still in place while Andre had been bowled out quite quickly.

Now it was our turn, again our team said that we could bat first, 'Not if you want to win,' I said 'I never was any good at cricket at school.'

'Don't worry young man; your name's Kris isn't it? It's only a bit of fun, get out there lad.' So Todd and I donned a pair of pads, no head protection in those days, and took to the field. Todd wasn't bad, he hit the first ball for a four, then a couple of balls later we managed another run. This meant that I was now in the crease dreading the first ball. Brian proved to be as an accomplished a bowler as he was a batsman and bypassed my bat to smash the stumps out of the ground.

'Howzat!' came the cry from the other team, a blessed release as far as I was concerned and made my way back to the pavilion where the ginger beer was waiting. After half an hour Brian had managed to unseat a couple more and his team were declared the winners.

'That means the beers are on us.' Said the team captain, who had been on the other side, 'so, show time!'

'Beers?' I whispered to Todd, 'what odds do you give that we'll get any?'

'Evens,' he replied.

The pavilion was quite large with a small stage, probably for speeches rather than concerts, at one end. The wives and girlfriends of the team members had now arrived armed with heaps of sandwiches, pork pies, my favourite, sausage rolls, another favourite and all kinds of pickles, salads and bread. I was reminded of the song from 'Oliver', 'Food, Glorious Food', remember us Borstal boys hadn't seen much in the way of quality food for some time and we wanted to dive right in there.

'OK boys and girls,' the chairman of the club stood up on the stage 'let's grab a quick bite before these young lads show us what they can do eh?' He was, without any doubt, a Welshman, an accent like his you could not ignore. So, on his instructions we all grabbed ourselves a plate and proceeded to pile it high with all the goodies on offer.

'Beer lads?' The Welshman asked with an eyebrow raised, all eyes turned to Bernie King who looked as if he had been put on the spot.

'Well...........'

'Oh go on man, I'm not going to get them drunk am I, just a couple of cans each to help with lubricate the larynx so as to speak, what do you say?' Bernie looked embarrassed.

'All right, but not a word back at the camp or I'll have your guts for guitar strings, OK?'

'OK!' we roared in unison then the chairman handed us each a can, which, I at least, savoured. It went some way towards making up for the loss of the rhubarb wine.

While everyone was filling their face I made my way over to Bernie King.

'How did you manage to get us this gig then Sir?' I enquired.

'I sometimes do the scoring for them when they have a match at home; my brother in law is on the team.'

'I don't mind if we do a few more of these, maybe they'd like us to come back again next week?' That made him laugh, 'or do you score for anybody else?' that made him laugh even more but I was being serious.

We were all having a really good time so when it came to doing our show everyone was already in a relaxed mood. The show had changed a bit without Kevin being there to play his Latin American stuff. This leant the music side of things on my shoulders bit more. I did my usual selection of Lennon, Neil Young, Bob Dylan 'et al' on my own, and then Todd joined me to play the blues jams that we played on the farm. I would make up words as we went along as well as playing stuff like 'Spoonful' and 'Hootchie Cootchie Man'. Brian and Andre worked their way through their comedy routines, which I have to say had improved considerably since we first started all those months ago.

All in all I think we gave them a good show.

When we had finished and went back to get some more food and another can of beer, the Chairman stood up on the stage. I thought he was going to make a speech of some kind, well, he did that first.

'On behalf of all the club members I would like to thank these lads for a stupendous evening, I particularly enjoyed the blues. Now I am sure you all know I come from Wales.' This brought a mixture of laughs and groans 'and I'm sure you all know I used to sing in the pit choir where I worked.' That brought more groans than laughs this time 'so I want to sing something for you now, 'Men of Harlech.'

I don't know what it is about the Welsh, lovely people but why do they all think they can sing? Maybe some of you remember Harry Secombe? He was a comedian, actor, all round entertainer back in the fifties to the seventies, he was Welsh. He started in a radio show called 'The Goon Show' with Spike Milligan and Peter Sellers, he was great in that. I used to listen to it on my transistor radio under the bed covers when I was a kid. Then he decided he could sing as well, and ended up in 'Oliver' as Mr Bumble, he was ok but..............

I like 'Men of Harlech' it's a rousing song that I believe the Welsh regiment sang at Rourke's Drift when the Zulus were about to carve them up. I was dreading his rendition, as it would seem, did most of the cricket club members. In all fairness when he struck up, totally unaccompanied, I thought he did a passable version of the song. It was then that I realised that it was his party piece and that everyone there enjoyed what he did, they were just pulling his leg.

I think that evening was the best gig we played as the entertainments committee, and sadly the last. Well with the line up that performed that night anyway as, other than Todd, the rest of us had been there a while and would be released sooner rather than later. I guessed that Todd wouldn't carry on once I'd left, I don't know if he did or not.

The time had come to leave and we said all our goodbyes to the very nice people who we had spent the evening with. They had treated us like equals and not convicts who they should lock their valuables away from. Having said that, none of the shows we played treated us like that, we were always given a warm welcome.

So back on the bus it was, I think we arrived back a little later than we should have done. Lights were out, although no one was asleep. Bernie had once more sworn us to secrecy with regards to the two cans of beer each of us had consumed. However I was grilled by the dorm on my return about whether I'd had a drink or not, needless to say I made them jealous with the tales of beer and pies. I knew Bernie wouldn't get into any trouble, it was probably par for the course and expected so I slept soundly with a clear conscience.

++++++++++++++

June was, as the old song goes, busting out all over, weather was fab and we were marching on towards another tie board. Kevin had finally made it to his discharge, he was a strange dude but I would miss him. Harry Norton, our intrepid dorm leader, went into the discharge unit for his last two weeks to be replaced by Alan Welch, a very good choice I thought. I'm not so sure many others felt the same but he was ok really. What came as a bigger surprise to me was the choice of his deputy, yours truly, I was gob smacked. Not that deputy dorm leader meant much; it didn't even guarantee I would take over when Pete went.

The atmosphere in the dorm was one of peace and tranquillity; even Winston had settled in, there had been no more trouble for him since the incident with J2, thankfully. Generally there was very little trouble at all in the entire Borstal, my vendetta with J.J an exception of course but I think only he, Phil and I knew it.

With my home leave looming I had to have a visit from my probation office. He had already gone to visit Moira in Earls Court but hadn't given her any indication of what his decision would be. So on the day of my meeting with him I had to go to the housemaster's office. Suffice to say I was really, really nervous, not knowing what to expect. I sat down in front of him; I didn't think he looked like the friendly kind, he wasn't.

'I've been to see your, er fiancée' no hello, how are you or any kind of greeting and I could tell from his attitude that he didn't really believe Moira was my intended. 'I'm not sure that this is the best place for you to be going on your home leave.' I went cold, I thought that this had been a done deal and the path had been smoothed for me to go there.

'I'm sorry,' I spluttered, 'I don't understand what the problem is, I have already spoken to Mr Hawks about this and he didn't seem to think there would be a problem.'

'Well Mr Hawks does not make the decisions about these things, I do.'

Had this been when I first came into Gaynes Hall I would have shut my mouth and let him walk all over me, but not today.

'Well, with all due respect Mr?' I left my words hanging in the air, waiting for him to actually tell me his name, a few seconds passed.

'Bailey, my name is Bailey.'

'Well MISTER Bailey, with all due respect, perhaps you would be so kind as to tell me what the problem is with my going to stay with my fiancée? I was living together with her for the best part of a year before coming here so, why not?'

'I don't consider one room to be an adequate environment for you to be staying in.'

'How many rooms do I need for five days?'

'You're a very insubordinate young man aren't you?'

'No sir, I'm just standing up for myself, there is nothing wrong with either my fiancée or where she is living. I will be living there, when I am eventually released, so what difference does it make if I go there on home leave?'

'I think you will be better off at your parent's house.'

'Why and have you actually been there?'

'No I haven't.'

'Then how do you know that their house is suitable?' that one stumped him for a few seconds, and then he sidestepped it.

'There is a lot less chance of you getting into any trouble whilst staying at your parents' house.'

'And what makes you think I will get into any trouble whilst I stay with my fiancee?'

'There is more chance of it happening if you do.'

'I resent that! I am not a habitual criminal, you have no evidence that I will do anything whilst I am there.' I paused for a moment to contain my anger; I didn't want to give him any other reason for blocking my home leave with Moira. 'Look, Mr Bailey, I know you have no reason to trust me but I don't want to come back here in the future or any other of Her Majesties fine establishments. So I have no intention of doing anything that might upset my eventual release. I want to spend my home leave with my girlfriend, I will of course visit my parents as well but I *do not* want to spend the entire five days with them.'

He was quite for a few moments.

'I will inform you of my decision in a few days, you can go now.'

'Thank you,' I left the room boiling with anger, the idea of having to go to see this piece of shit for two years after I was released made it even worse. I vowed that I would go to see Ron Hawks as soon as possible; I always felt that he was on my side. I did just that on the very same day. He was very sympathetic to my concerns but said there was very little he could do other than recommend that I should go to Moira's. It was only a matter of days before Hawks called me into his office to tell me that the probation service had approved where I would be going on my home leave. What a relief, although, had they forced me to go to my parents I would have gone to stay with Moira anyway, I can't imagine ma and pa would have made too much of a fuss.

+++++++++++++++

One day as I was returning to the dorm after my usual late breakfast Ron Hawks came out of his office to call me in.

'Step into my office a moment will you Gray?'

'Certainly Sir,' I thought it must be something to do with my home leave.

'Where is your guitar, the one you had sent in?'

'Up at the farm sir, why?'

'Mr Hunt, who has been wading his way through one of your young lady's epic sagas, seems to think that it may be elsewhere.'

I didn't know what he was talking about.

'I'm sorry Sir, I don't understand.'

'In this letter she makes a reference to your father collecting your guitar and taking it home with him, when did this happen?'

For a few moments I was totally baffled, then it came to me.

'I have more than one guitar Sir, one of them is quite expensive and I think Moira was concerned about it being at her flat. Perhaps she has given it to my father for safe keeping.'

I could see that this scenario hadn't occurred to him and he looked a little embarrassed.

'Perhaps you could bring it back today, just to set my mind at rest?'

'Of course Sir.'

Not only was I using it to sooth the savage beasts whilst they delivered their milk, I was also giving Gibbons young son and daughter guitar lessons. He'd called me into his office one day after hearing me serenading the herd one afternoon. He offered me some tobacco for doing this but, to be honest, with the extras I was smuggling in on visits every week and what I could buy with my increased wages as an STG, I didn't need it. However, that didn't stop me obliging him on the promise of a can of beer every time I gave them a lesson. It was also a good grovel, it couldn't hurt my report from him, although I did wonder if he would want to keep me there just to carry on the lessons............. Nah!

I dutifully took the guitar back to the dorm that afternoon, needless to say Hawks was satisfied and I took it back again the next day. It was spending more time on the farm these days anyway, I didn't like to play in the evenings unless specifically asked to do so, which I was now and then.

It was a bit chaotic up on the farm in June as we had a civilian company in to tear down and rebuild the Dutch barn whilst the herd was in the field during the summer months. Although they were at the other end of the farm we still had to bring the herd past the building site, which at times, was a bit of a mess. Fraternisation between Borstal boys and civilian workers was not encouraged, in case they smuggled in contraband, like tobacco and alcohol. I didn't want to get involved in any contraband, I didn't really need it, but I know there were some who did. That didn't mean I didn't speak to any of them, I did but only idle chitchat, you can always find someone to talk about music.

It was around this time that my old sparing partner J.J was about to be discharged. He'd been in the discharge unit for just over a week when Phil went out on his home leave. I guessed that this would afford him an opportunity to have his last pop at me, I wasn't wrong.

One afternoon he wandered around to the milking shed when Todd had gone off to bring in the herd, knowing I would be alone.

I was prepared for his visit and had seen him pass the door where the cows left the milking shed. I looked around for a weapon; there were plenty of things I could use including a lump wood lying in the corner. This was a legacy of my South African predecessor who used to enjoy beating the cows with it as you may remember. It was in my hand as he came through the door.

'What do you want?' I asked as he stopped in his tracks when he saw what I had in my hand. 'Come to say goodbye and wish me good luck?'

'You wouldn't dare to use that,' he sneered at me, 'you haven't got the bottle.'

'Try me,' I answered 'I'm not the timid recepo I used to be, you start it, I'll finish it. When are you going home? You've got two days and an early? Do you really want to stay here for a bit longer just to have a pop at me? Had to wait till Phil was out the way though didn't you? So fuck off back to your job, fuck off back to Exeter on Wednesday and have a thoroughly unpleasant life.'

'If I ever see you on the out you piece of sh..'

'You wont,' I interrupted 'I don't have any plans to come to Exeter and I don't suppose you could ever find London.' I could see that he dearly wanted to take a swing at me but together with the lump of wood in my hand and fact that he could loose his discharge, he turned on his heel and stomped out.

'Fuck you Gray!' he shouted as his parting shot.

'Yeah and fuck you too,' I said calmly but I think he was out of earshot by the time.

+++++++++++++++

Finally the 22nd of June came around, time for the tie board and I was up on my first month as an STG. Suffice to say I was nervous and expectant, I believed that I had grovelled all I could grovel and shown that I was a totally reformed character ready to go back out into the world.

Unfortunately the powers that be didn't agree. I stood before Ron Hawkes, Bob Lewis and some cast iron knickers wearer from the board of visitors. Hawkes looked up at me from the paper work in front of him and smiled.

'Gray, you've been one month as an STG and I have had glowing reports from Mr Gibbons and Mr O'Reilly at the farm and a number of other officers. However I'm sorry to say that, this month, we are unable to award your discharge.' I went cold; I really thought that I had it in the bag. 'Mr Lewis particularly thought that you could benefit from a little bit longer.'

'Bastard!' I thought, after all the sucking up I'd done with him as well!

'Yes Sir, thank you Sir.' I turned on my heels and left the room fighting to keep back the tears, I didn't want any of the other lads to see that it was getting to me. I think I gave off the impression that I was convinced that I would get my discharge and I had been taken down a peg or two by not getting it. I wasn't alone in my disappointment of course but at least Russell finally received his STG. Bizarrely one of the lads on my reception party went straight from his red to brown and a first date release, we never did find out why. Phil also got his discharge.

Thankfully no one gave me a hard time about not getting my discharge and I settled back into the dorm nursing my wounds. It was also still almost three weeks until my home leave. I was more than a little depressed; I had really set my sights on getting a release date before I went on home leave. I had to accept that this was now no longer going to happen. I also knew that Moira would be on the phone later to see if I had got it, I knew she would be as disappointed as I was now. I wished that I could speak to her, try and let her see that it wasn't that bad, I was sure to get it next time, wasn't I?

That weekend we had a real treat, a film, The Virgin Soldiers; it was great to see a film. Not that it was the best film ever made but for someone who loves the movies and had been deprived for a number of months, this was a breath of fresh air. The film was less than a year old having been released in the cinema in 1970. It wasn't like today, on to DVD in less than three months and TV in less than six, oh no, no such thing as video or DVD and at least three years before it hit TV.

It helped to take the edge off the disappointment.

++++++++++++++++

Meanwhile, back on the farm I was keeping up appearances as the keen farmer who couldn't wait to get to agricultural college. I was also writing furiously to possible employers, like the milk marketing board and the artificial insemination centre I had visited. Although the idea of spending most of my life with my arm thrust up a cows fanny didn't really appeal. I wasn't against thrusting anything else up a fanny, but not a cow's; although in hindsight that is something I probably did, just a different kind of cow.

The two legged variety.

J.J had finally gone and Phil was on his home leave; when he came back he was late having lost his return ticket and missed the train trying to find it. The staff were not amused and confiscated all his tobacco as a punishment, I couldn't help but laugh, it could only have happened to him, although I thought it was somewhat petty to take all his burn, at least he came back!

There was a relatively new lad in the mill by the name of Pete; he hadn't been in the job very long when he had to be rushed to hospital with appendicitis. The rumours flew around the camp like a swarm of bees; he'd had an accident in the mill and lost a hand. Another one was that he'd had a bad fall and had died. It was quite amusing to hear some of the suggestions as to what had happened. In fact the truth was that he had been feeling sick and was suffering from a bad pain in his side. Gibbons had taken him to see the doctor in the village, as the one on the camp wasn't in attendance on that particular day.

There were very few accidents of any kind either on the farm or on the camp in general. Very few, I said, however, one of the very few happened to me. It was one morning during milking, I don't really know how it happened but as I was letting one of the beasties out after draining her of milk the gate swung back and closed on my right thumb. Boy did it hurt; I almost lost consciousness with the pain, which after a while subsided to a low aching throb. As the day progressed the pain didn't seem to get any easier and I had a dreadful nights sleep because of it. I should have gone to see matron at least as soon as I could after it happened, but........

By the next morning my thumb had swollen to twice its normal size and my nail had gone completely black. There was no avoiding the matron now, so after the morning milk I went to see her. Again the doctor would only come in on certain days, although he was on call for emergencies. This however was not deemed an emergency and Jim Hunt, who was duty officer that day, took me to the hospital.

After about an hour or so a nurse took me into a cubicle where she inspected my injury, she didn't think it was broken, despite the swelling but would send me for an X-ray anyway. This took about another hour or so and was now way past lunch and would soon be coming up to afternoon milking. I knew Phil and Todd could manage but I didn't like leaving them to do it on their own.

The X-ray, as the nurse had correctly diagnosed, revealed no fracture to my thumb but it would be necessary to remove the nail as it was now dead. I didn't like the sound of that as I was sure that it would mean pain, something I try to avoid at all costs. I was expecting a doctor to come and do the deed but my friendly nurse came back and injected my thumb four or five times with a local anaesthetic. I barely felt the needle because she was very good with it. I hate needles, could never have become a junkie, so was pleased she was gentle in her technique.

Very quickly I lost all feeling in the thumb, then, the doctor came and removed the nail in no time at all whilst I looked away. I always look away, it helps. I never felt a thing, thankfully, then my little nurse came back to dress the wound, which I would have to change every day. I felt fine until an hour or so later when the anaesthetic started to wear off, then I started to feel serious pain. I went back to matron, who gave me a couple of aspirin, which, needless to say, did very little to ease it. I had another restless night; it took quite a few days before it became bearable and quite sometime before the nail grew back again.

At about the same time as my injury my favourite member of the herd, Jo, managed to get a serious case of mastitis. That is when they get an infection in the udder, which curdles the milk that they are producing. This, naturally, makes it unfit for human consumption but you still have to milk her. Then once you have done this the machine must be emptied out the bottom, obviously not into the tank. Then the whole machine has to be cleaned and disinfected so the poor thing had to be the last one to be milked.

After she had been drained of her milk I had to inject something to help cure the infection straight into her teat. This was probably quite unpleasant for the poor cow and not a lot of fun for me either. Especially as she wouldn't let anyone else do it. Unfortunately things got worse, there was more to the problem than mastitis and she eventually had to have a small operation on the teat to remove a growth inside.

The vet came to perform the surgery with a local anaesthetic, just like my thumb and me. She trusted me and I felt awful that I had to be part of something that caused her distress. First I kept her back after the milking then, when the vet arrived, took her into a stable where he gave her a mild sedative to keep her a bit calmer. When she started to get a bit shaky on her legs I helped her to lie down. The vet then injected her teat with the local whilst I stroked her head and spoke to her like she was a baby.

It didn't take long to remove the growth but I stayed in the stable until the sedative started to wear off. We kept her there for another week; the vet showed me how to change the dressing, which I did every day. Later she was returned to the herd and continued to give her milk for the breakfast cereals and cups of tea of the people of England.

++++++++++++++++

June had slipped into July and the days were getting longer, it was still daylight when we went to bed at ten. Not that it worried me I was always ready to sleep long before ten; in fact I was often in by nine, due to the inhospitably early hour I had to get up. Normally I would be up at four, just as the dawn's early light was breaking but one morning when the night watchman woke me it was still dark outside.

'Cows are loose laddie,' he whispered 'Mr Gibbons wants you to meet him at the field where they should be, they're all over the place.'

'Oh great,' I thought 'just what I need right now, to chase a bunch of marauding cows through the countryside!'

It was almost three in the morning when I heaved myself out of bed to get dressed. By the time I arrived at the field, where the herd should have been, Phil and Todd had already arrived and with Paddy were waiting for me.

'Mr Gibbons'll be here soon,' he said 'but you boys take these torches and make a start, dare are all over the fooking place. It'll be light in an hour or so which will make it a lot easier if we haven't penned them by then.' Have them penned in an hour? I think he was being a bit more than optimistic; some of the buggers were more than a mile away.

I doubt that you have ever had the need to chase a cow but trust me they can run, don't be fooled by all that bulk. With no horses to ride around on, not that I would have been able to ride one, nor any dog that could have rounded them up like sheep, this was no Wild West show featuring cowboys with lassos, oh no. There was just we three, not so hairy, Borstal boys, a middle aged farmer and an over weight Irishman lumbering around the countryside.

We managed to bring back the bulk of the herd in less than an hour, but, of course there were the few stubborn beasties who managed to drag out the round up well into the morning. The trick was not to run after them because as soon as you did that they would be on their toes long before you could get anywhere near. No, the idea was to creep slowly around the front of the animal then gently coax it in the direction you wanted it to go. As I said, most of them would go willingly and of course the ones who wouldn't would also be the furthest away.

I still have this very vivid picture in my mind of Todd racing after one of the beasties, yelling all kinds of obscenities in the vain hope that it would do the right thing and stop. Sadly it didn't, I couldn't help as I had enough problems of my own with another pair who wouldn't play ball.

The younger ones were the worst of course, aren't they always, no matter what kind of animal? I think I must have covered miles that morning rounding up the last absconders; I could easily have disappeared myself. By the time they were all safely in the yard we didn't start milking until well into the morning. We'd long missed breakfast but Paddy had managed to have some sandwiches made for us. Lunch was also late because we were still milking when it started, but we did get some even if it was late. We were given most of the afternoon off to recover and because of the late morning milking session we put the afternoon one back a couple of hours.

I'm pretty sure I was in bed and sound asleep long before lights out, I was shattered. Despite the aggravation the breakout had caused us all there were a number of moments when I couldn't stop myself from laughing. Watching Todd loose a race with a cow was one and Paddy waving his stick around because he couldn't run anywhere was another. We all fell over more than once by either slipping in mud or a cow pat; thankfully I never managed to land in one like Phil did.

Did I really want to spend my life doing things like this?

Nah!

+++++++++++++++++

Home leave was drawing ever nearer, slowly, but surely the fifteenth of July was coming my way. I had made a makeshift calendar that I had named 'Calendar 'a la' Bird' on which I had noted all of the tie board dates. This had been colour coded to reflect the ties and I dutifully crossed off every day in the evening.

Two weeks before I went on home leave my friend and saviour Phil was discharged; I was really upset, as we had been very close. We swore to keep in touch, but…….. And, on that day Alan Welch, our dorm leader, went into the discharge unit so I was promoted to dorm leader. What surprised me more than a little bit was their choice for my deputy, Russell, he was brave enough to face up to people but no one took any notice. When I went on home leave he would be in charge and I wasn't sure how that would sit with the rest of the dorm. Before I left I had a quiet word with the most likely suspects to give him trouble. I said that it would reflect on me if they gave him problems and that would displease me considerably. I think all went well; I didn't get any tales of woe from him or anyone else when I returned.

One of the very few privileges of being dorm leader was being able to have a watch. All my personal belongings that I'd had when I'd been sent down had gone home with my clothes when dad took them. So he had to bring it back for me, it wasn't much but it made you feel like you were someone. Sad eh?

Being dorm leader made one important change in my routine; I now had to be present for Saturday morning inspection. I hadn't been present for one of those for months and it was going to be a bit of a chore for me. I was determined that my first inspection as dorm leader was going to go without a hitch. It was strange getting up at the same time as everyone else once a week.

When Phil was discharged I was given a new number three, Sid Buckworth, who had been on the same reception party as me and had been working on the farm party ever since. Sid was a decent enough bloke, just not the sharpest tool in the box. Just as well Todd knew what he was doing as not only did they have to manage on Saturday mornings without me they would need to manage for almost a week when I went on home leave.

So the first Saturday morning came and I had made up my list of jobs and who was going to do them, I received no arguments from anyone. I warned that anyone who let me down would be on bathhouse duty until I left. Each dorm had to take it in turns to clean the bathhouse that was situated between J2 and J3 on a weekly turnaround. Usually it was the most junior members of the dorm who performed this task. I didn't care if it was Russell or any other senior member of the dorm, if they let me down on the first week they would suffer.

That first morning everyone seemed to be working the elbow grease furiously, I was no exception. My bed space, now one of the coveted corner spaces that had been mine for a couple of weeks before my promotion, shone like a diamond. I constantly walked up and down the centre deck looking over everyone's shoulder to see that they weren't slacking. Nobody was, then, when all was finished everyone was herded outside whilst the centre deck was polished and buffed.

Everyone had to wait outside until Ron Hawks and Bob Lewis came to inspect us. J1 was always the first, being nearest to the office, that could either work for us or against us. Either they forgot how bad we were by the time they got to J4 or forgot how good we were. I was really nervous as we all filed back into the dorm and stood at ease. Hawks and Lewis waited at the door whilst I brought the dorm to attention.

'J1, J1 attenshun!' after everyone had snapped to attention I invited the two members of staff to come in.

'At ease J1.' Hawks ordered, I was expected to follow them both as they made their way down the centre deck, inspecting each boy's locker, kit and bed space. Lewis naturally made a few minor remarks about one or two of the kits but no really bad complaints.

'Not a bad start Gray,' Hawks said as he was leaving, 'keep it up.' Lewis didn't say anything, just gave me a kind of sideways smile, which worried me somewhat. As they closed the door everyone sighed with relief, me in particular, and started to roll a cigarette.

'Thank fuck that's over,' I said 'well done everyone I think we got away with it!' Got away with it we most certainly had, not only had we got away with it we also won the shield for the best dorm of the week.

How a-fucking-bout that?

I don't know if it was just because it was my first inspection but I doubt it. All I know is that I was glad it was all over and I hadn't ended up with egg on my face, I gave everyone a burn as a 'thank you' for a good job, hoping it would encourage them next time, they always did a great job and I was always proud of them.

++++++++++++++++

In the second week of July, just as I took over as dorm leader, Ron Hawks called me into the office. He informed me that we were to become host to a university student from Cambridge who was studying the prison and Borstal system. He wouldn't be alone; there were another four who would be scattered around the camp. It was thought that J1 and I would be the right place, as we could be trusted to look after them. That made me feel pretty good, out of twelve dorms in the three houses; mine was considered one of the best for them to be in.

So before James arrived I had a pep talk with the dorm.

'Tomorrow we are having a guest in the dorm, he's a student from Cambridge University who has come to see the Borstal system at first hand. There are five students in total and we have been chosen as one of the dorms to accommodate them because **we can be trusted!** Now, if anyone let's me down they will most certainly wish they had never come to this dorm!' I don't really know what I could have done but I had to threaten something.

'I don't want any practical jokes, no apple pie beds or telling them they have to take fire extinguishers on parade with them, understand? They are going to go away with wondering why such a nice bunch of lads are doing time, OK?' Everyone nodded in agreement but there were still one or two of our ensemble that worried me, especially Jock.

When James arrived after dinner,(don't know if I ever knew his other name,) I was called over to the main office to be his sponsor and bring him back to the dorm. I think he was a little bit more than nervous, he probably had the same impression of Borstal that I'd had before I arrived there.

After we had been introduced we went to the stores get his kit for the short stay. Once we had that it was the short stroll back to J1.

'Have you been here long?' he asked as we made our way over to it.

'Since the end of January' I replied

'So what is it like here?'

'It's all right I suppose, I expected a lot worse.' I knew I had to be careful what I said; he wasn't after all, one of us. 'Have you been to the Scrubs as well?' I asked.

'No, just here.'

'Lucky you, I understand you are studying the Borstal system, is this for your degree?'

'I'm studying criminal law, I want to be a criminal lawyer.'

'Well, there are a few criminals here for you to study mate!'

'I, don't want to study you guys, I want to study the system' he sounded worried that we were going to be aggressive towards him.

'Don't worry James, they're all decent lads who just want to do their bird and get back home, they wont give you any trouble.'

'I, didn't mean….'

'It'll be all right, trust me.' I'm not sure that he believed me. 'There's just one thing I would recommend you don't do.'

'And that is?'

'Don't keep asking them what they are in for, if they volunteer the information, ok but most of us are sick and tired of that question.'

'No problem, thanks for the heads up.'

We had to make room for a bed for James, which was quite easy, we had a depleted number in J1 due to the lack of an influx of Borstal boys over the past couple new arrivals. A bed, with straps rather than springs, so he would understand what a new arrival would experience, was brought in for him.

Everyone in the dorm was waiting eagerly for his arrival, he must have felt like Royalty when I first brought him in. they were almost falling over themselves to help him settle in to his bed space whilst doing their best to explain what he could and couldn't do.

Once again I was proud of them.

The evening passed easily with more questions being asked of him than the other way around. He seemed a likeable enough guy, the same age group as all of us, which made it a lot easier to deal with him. It didn't take him long to settle in and feel at ease with us.

Of course we had to have a round of the 'boat vote', especially for James' benefit. It had been a while since I had been the major target for being voted out, Jock still liked to vote for me. It never bothered me that he did this, I guess he thought as I had been his sponsor and was now dorm leader he could get away with it. He did, I was long passed caring about who voted me out and who didn't but most were afraid of being put on some shit detail if they upset me. I could have bet that nearly everyone in the dorm would vote James out but I doubt the odds would have been good. I didn't vote him out but I think most of the others did, I did reassure him in the morning that this was normal and he shouldn't worry about it.

Because James was with us for three nights I had to leave early morning milking to Todd and Sid. Todd was a good number two so I didn't have any problems leaving it to him, especially as he would have to cope when I went on my home leave.

James stuck to me like glue as we went to breakfast. The Cambridge lads didn't congregate together in the dining room but stayed with their various dorms. I had to show him how to bumper his bed-space and lay his kit out. An officer could come and inspect the dorm at any time and if it wasn't up to scratch there would be some kind of penalty meted out them. He threw himself into the task with more then enough vigour that put some of the others to shame. Still, he didn't have to do it for months on end, did he?

The next evening was dorm agro night, hosted by Ken Forshaw; of course James was the centre of attraction.

'So what do you think you have gained from being here James?' someone asked him

'The knowledge that I never should commit a crime.' That made everyone laugh, and eased the atmosphere somewhat. James told us more about himself and his family, I don't remember anything he said but he definitely came over as a truly nice guy. He assured us all that he wanted to be able to defend rather than prosecute, which endeared him to everyone even more.

His three days passed quickly and off he went back to university. I don't know if he become a defence lawyer but I like to think he did.

* * * * *

Chapter five
I'm Sittin' In A Railway Station, Got a Ticket For My Destination

After one hundred and seventy one days, and an early (that means the breakfast on the day you leave) I was finally awaiting the transport that would take me to the station in Huntingdon. It had been fifty days, and an early since I had received my green tie and home-leave date. Home-leave was every two weeks on a Thursday, I was given the second date so had to wait that much longer before it was my turn.

From Huntingdon, along with a number of other lucky lads, I would catch a train to Kings Cross where, hopefully, Moira would be waiting for me. I can't remember how many others there were or who was going with me but I do know that we were all revved up and ready to go.

My home leave had started.

It was marred somewhat by the shocked disappointment of not having received my brown tie and the much yearned for discharge date. I had hoped to know when I would be going home for the last time as I set foot on the train for home leave, but it was not to be. I was; however, fairly confident that I would get my brown at the next tie board that was only a week after my return. Still, I wasn't going to let it dampen my euphoria at breathing in free air too much.

My parents had long ago taken home the clothes that I was wearing when I'd been sent down so I waited in the library for the mini bus dressed in my wonderful discharge suit. It wasn't really that uncomfortable but, whilst wearing it I could not be accused of being a dedicated follower of fashion. It was going to be bad enough walking from Earls Court tube station to Longridge Road, -hopefully without being seen-, so there was no way I would be strutting my stuff along the Kings Road in it!

In no time we arrived at the station and boarded the train. We had been issued with return tickets, mine all the way to Earls Court. There was a buffet car on the train, but in those days they were not allowed to sell alcohol outside of licensing hours, which at nine in the morning it most certainly was. So I settled for a cup of tea whilst others enjoyed a coke, something I never have done, well not the liquid kind anyway.

It seemed to take forever before we arrived at Kings Cross, stopping at probably every station on the way, but I didn't care, I was free, albeit for only five days, but free none the less.

The end was in sight

Talking of sights, there was a wonderful sight waiting for me by the barrier at the end of the platform. Moira, in the most skimpy hot pant suit possible, hot pants were the height of fashion back in 1971. If her intention had been to raise my blood pressure I can tell you it worked. Remember I hadn't had sex for the best part of six months and, trust me I was ready for it. If she had been standing there in a sack I would have felt the same, horny. It was great to see her without being in a room full of other Borstal boys and some screw looking over your shoulder to make sure she wasn't playing with my dick! Which, she had done on a number of occasions when she had come to visit.

A lot of the time, during visits, the presiding officer would be in the office rather than standing in the visiting room all day. So we could canoodle a little bit, which often progressed to a little petting and sometime even a bit of heavy petting. During one of these heavy petting sessions, as my eyes were watering and I was just about to make a mess in my underwear, a soft voice said.

'I think you should both calm down a bit, this isn't the right place for a love in!' it was the presiding officer of the day. I think Moira and I had been getting just a bit to intimate without realising it. I still cringe at the memory, even today. So now, on the 15th July 1971 we were shaking tongues on the platform at Kings Cross Station before hurrying home to Earls Court for something far more intense!

++++++++++++++++

It's difficult to describe the sensation that I felt as we made our way down to the tube station, apart from the joy of being free that is. My head was swimming in way that it had never done before, in a short time I realised it was the hustle and bustle of people passing me by. I'd spent the last six months in a quiet environment with no cars, trains or buses and very few people. It was making me feel high, in a strange kind of way; it lasted for a couple of days, every time I went out into a crowd. I would have the same sensation on release as well.

The moment we stepped through the door of Moira's humble bed-sitting room our clothes came off to be strewn all over the floor as we fell together naked onto the bed. It had been a while and needless to say was over in a matter of seconds, but we did have five days to make up for it.

The room was much as you would imagine a double bed-sitting room to be, double bed in the corner, a sink, a small cooker with two hot plates and a grill, but no oven. There were also two ancient armchairs and a gas fire that you would need a pile of tanner's (an old pre decimal sixpence, worth two and a half new pence) to feed the meter with. Thankfully, as it was mid July we didn't need the fire but the cooker ran on gas as well. It wasn't ideal but it was home for Moira and would be home for both of us one day when I was released. Thankfully the probation officer who had to pass it fit for my home leave was, eventually, impressed enough to do so. The alternative would have been to spend the entire five days at my parent's house that would not have been as much fun. A visit to Romford was planned for Sunday; I hoped it wouldn't be spoilt by any arguments over the wedding plans.

Moira had taken four days leave from her job to be with me all the time I was home. So after our tumble in the sack I hung up my suit, not to be seen again until the time came for me to return, and put on my jeans and T-shirt. I still have a photograph taken on the steps of the house in Longridge Road during my home-leave, boy I look so young and handsome, what went wrong?

So that afternoon we went shopping for some food in the local supermarket, Macfisheries, do you remember them? Long gone I'm afraid, taken over by someone else, Tesco's probably. Our friend and neighbour, Beryl, worked there. She was a chubby, bubbly girl of about twenty-one who would be one of Moira's bridesmaids when we were married. When I walked into the store she was working on one of the checkouts and hadn't seen me coming in. After we'd finished shopping I queued up on my own so that Beryl wouldn't see Moira.

Beryl didn't look up from the items on the conveyor belt as she punched the prices into the till.

'How are you today Beryl?' I asked quietly, she looked puzzled for a split second, then....

'Kris!!!' she stood up and flung her arms around me, 'I, I didn't recognise you, your hair, you look....... Oh give me a kiss.' A few people behind me were getting a little impatient. 'Oh behave you lot, I haven't seen him for months.' She barked at the complaining queue, 'I finish work at four, I'll be around later, I think Moira has asked a few people to come around tonight.'

'OK babe,' I replied 'it's really great to see you, can't wait till later.'

Beryl gave me one last peck on the cheek before Moira appeared from nowhere to help me with the shopping after which we made our way back home.

That evening some friends came around to our humble abode. First to arrive was Cecil; he was one of the first musicians I had played with in Earls Court. I had answered an ad in the Melody Maker way back then, just after I left school. It was that ad that brought me to Earls Court, they needed a singer and Cecil was the lead guitarist. So I played rhythm and sang, then there was Dave on keyboards and Alan on bass, he would be along a bit later. Our problem was always a drummer; with or without a drummer they are always a problem.

Cecil was from Mauritius and his father was some big wig in their government. He knew how I was feeling having spent some time in jail after being involved in a burglary with a friend of his. Burglary wasn't really his scene, Cecil wasn't the criminal kind but his mate, Ronnie had dragged him into it. Thankfully, because it was his first offence, Cecil avoided jail time and received only probation. Ronnie on the other hand had previous so was sent to prison.

We also made one record together as Grobbert and Duff. It sold bugger all at the time but it has become a psychedelic cult classic. It can be found today on a couple of compilations of obscure psychedelic tracks of the sixties and seventies. It's a shame I eventually lost contact with him and all the others from those days in Earls Court. But of course there were no emails, mobile phones; texting in those days and not everyone had a phone.

Cecil would be my best man on the big day.

Today he brought two guitars with him; I didn't have one as my acoustic was at Gaynes Hall awaiting my return and my prized Rickenbacker, which I still have, was in Romford at my parents' house. He was a great guitar player and songwriter but a crap singer, but what a sweet gentle man. My father, initially, was against him being my best man, only because he was black, but he eventually warmed to him after we had a few beers together.

Ces' also brought a nice little piece of Lebanese red, which I promptly proceeded to roll into a nice little joint for the three of us. I used to love rolling joints, I considered it an art form, I could even make them a foot long and stable, without falling apart. This was really good stuff, I always liked the Lebanese cannabis, which came in red or gold, I wasn't fussy which. The first joint, shared just between the three of us, knocked my socks off and set the mood for the next five days.

So then Alan came, with his guitar, but Alan was super straight, he liked a beer but smoking dope was a no, no. I admired him for that really, didn't smoke it just because everyone else did, a very together guy. It was Alan I first shared a room with. When I home he was sharing with a friend he had come to London with, they were from Leeds. I slept on the floor for about a month before Adrian, the old friend, moved out of their room and in with his girlfriend. So I then progressed from the floor to a bed and started paying half the rent, £3.10s.0d that was close to half of my wages from the Post Office, but I didn't have my father going head to head with me everyday about my hair, my sideboards, my music taste and just about everything else to do with the youth culture of the day.

Alan was cool and Geordie Neil, another great guitar player, closely followed his arrival. His style was more Bert Jansch, a finger picker, I liked to play finger picking style too but Neil had it really nailed, he's brought some good puff as well, Afghan black, I was going to be seriously stoned by the end of the day. Neil and I had gravitated towards each other at Elektra House, the home of overseas telegraphs in the days before fax machines and email when people sent telegrams to each other. I spotted him as a head easily; I guess the long hair and the poncho kind of gave him away. He was from Newcastle upon Tyne and shared a flat with some other guys from work in Wandsworth.

We used to take a lot of acid together, he would have been my first choice as a best man but Neil was a bit flaky and could never have got it together, not that Ces' was on the ball either but a bit more together than Neil. He would eventually move in with Alan and I when we expanded to two rooms, one for sleeping and a lounge on the next floor, that was before I met Moira.

I wish I knew where Cecil, Alan and Neil are now.

So together with Cecil, Alan and Neil, plus Beryl and her flat mate Jenny we smoked our way through the Lebanese red, the Afghan black and drank all the beer I'd bought. The fours guitar players had jammed on songs ranging from The Beatles, The Rolling Stone, Donovan, Dylan, Bert Jansch, Pentangle, Jefferson Airplane, The Doors and many others I can't remember. We were all well stoned, so we decided to make our way to the Prince of Tek, my favourite watering hole in Earls Court, for a nightcap or three.

There was an upstairs bar that sold Directors Bitter, a great beer, where we made ourselves at home. I had by now put Gaynes Hall to the far corner of my mind; going back seemed such a long way off. I was pissed and stoned and amongst some of the best friends I had at the time, I was feeling good.

At closing time I bade farewell to them all then Moira steered me back to our love nest for a last fuck before I fell into a contented sleep.

My first night of freedom had been wonderful; I was looking forward to day two.

+++++++++++++++++

I slept like a log that night, although a bit groggy in the morning I was ready for the day Moira had planned for us. That consisted of spending the day in South Kensington at the Science and the Natural History Museums. I had first been there as a child with my grandfather. He loved London having been born, like his father and his father before him, on the Isle of Dogs, now part of Docklands. He'd shown me so much history of London when I was a small boy, the Tower, St Paul's, Westminster Abbey, all the museums and just about everywhere you can think of. I could make my way around the city with my eyes closed. Moira had never been to these museums and I hadn't been for a long time, it was great to see them again. In the future I would take my son there, I should go back again one day, its been a long time.

I forgot to mention that along with the Afghan black Neil had brought two tabs of acid,

Party time!

As I remember it the weather was hot and sunny that July and after we had tamped around the culture centre of South Ken we made our way up to Hyde Park where we dropped our tabs. I was remembering the last time I'd taken a trip in Hyde Park. A gang of us, including Moira, Neil and some other faces from the Earls Court Road went up to see a free concert. I'd been to a couple before, Blind Faith, The Rolling Stones but this time it was Pink Floyd, Roy Harper and The Edgar Broughton Band, little did I know I would end up working with them twenty odd years later.

That had been a hot day as well and by the time Floyd hit the stage I was tripping out of my gourde. Suddenly the crowd around me became a horde of riders on horseback, only the sound. As I closed my eyes I could hear thousands of hooves, thundering across Hyde Park. I didn't really hear Pink Floyd performing Atom Heart Mother, only the horses.

There were no horses there on this afternoon in Hyde Park, just Moira and I. Somehow I managed to block out anything I didn't want to hear, but I could hear the birds and the wind in the trees. Remember King Crimson 'I Talk to the Wind'? Well that day I felt as if I could talk to the wind.

Moira wouldn't let go of my hand and would ask me the time every few minutes. That's one effect that acid seems to have, it stretches time, what you think is an hour can be just a few minutes. I think we went all around Hyde Park that afternoon before walking back to Earls Court. It felt like the effects of the acid had worn off by the time we arrived back to our room. I was wrong; I had just grown accustomed to effects of the drug and the open air but the moment I stepped inside the house it came back like a sledgehammer.

I hadn't come down at all, no Sir!

My vision was all distorted and I could hear a record playing in another room but it was stuck in the groove, playing the same bit over and over again. In my hallucinating mind I thought that there was something wrong with the person in there so I went to knock on the door to see if I could help. A tall man looking the spitting image of the actor Peter Wyngard opened the door.

'What can eye do for yees?' he asked me in a very obvious gay Scottish accent.

'Is, is everything all right here?' I asked back 'it just sounded as if there was something wrong with your record player.'

'Everything is fine and dandy, are you sure there is nothing wrong with you?' and promptly closed the door. I felt a bit of a fool, especially as I realised the hallucinogenic that had been running around my body had been playing games with my mind, should have known it really. By a twist of events, when I was finally released, Dennis, the gay Scotsman, would become a good friend of both Moira and I. His sister was the cleaner of the house and she had a three-year-old daughter who was really cute and a bundle of laughs.

So, having made a complete fool of myself, we decided it might be best to lock ourselves away for the evening playing records. As a welcome home present Moira had bought the new double live album 'Four Way Street' by Crosby, Stills, Nash and Young. I'd been building up quite a list of albums that I intended to buy when I was home and free. These included Paul McCartney's Ram, The Rolling Stones - Sticky Fingers, Doors - LA Woman and The Strawbs – From the Witchwood. I didn't get them all right away, money was too tight to mention, but I still have them in my prized vinyl collection as well as copies on CD.

I think we finally went to sleep at about two or three in the morning, it had been a nice day. We'd had some culture in the museums, some adventures in Hyde Park and some fine music to round the day off.

+++++++++++++++

There was no rush to get out of bed on Saturday morning; we'd planned to go out to dinner that evening in my favourite local restaurant 'The Soo-Sol'. Sadly long gone but they did the most amazing devilled kidneys I have ever had and I was looking forward to having a large plate of them before the day was out. We had also planned to meet Neil and the gang in the Prince of Tek afterwards.

I don't know if it was just the come down from the acid but I was feeling quite depressed that morning and it was beginning to show. I was grumpy to say the very least, I'd been home two days and already I was thinking about having to go back. Nor was I really looking forward to going to see my parents on Sunday, not that I didn't want to see them; I just wasn't looking forward to any kind of discussion about the wedding. I can't really describe how I was feeling because it was so long ago; I just know that the euphoria of being free again mixed with the knowledge that the freedom was short lived was bringing me down. It didn't help that Moira didn't understand how I was feeling and I wasn't explaining myself very well. So I chose to roll over in bed, spurning her advances, and pretend to go back to sleep.

That didn't go down very well, so we had an argument, 'what was wrong with me?' She asked and I just didn't really know, didn't I want to make love to her? Well of course I did, so I just blamed the comedown from the acid but she was now in a bad mood for the rest of the morning and part of the afternoon.

When I finally made it out of bed around lunchtime we ventured out into the sun to go and have some coffee in the Troubadour in Old Brompton Road. In the future Cecil and I would run a little folk/music club in the basement where we would try out some of the songs we wrote on the audience there. This was where I met American folkie Tom Paxton who came to sing a few songs during a night off from his UK tour. I would also meet Mike Absalom, someone who I would be involved with as a bass player in the future, but that's another story for another time.

Gradually the ice between Moira and I melted until the time came to go and have the devilled kidneys I had been looking forward to for so long. Gaynes Hall food wasn't all bad but neither was it all good. I hadn't really had a proper meal since I'd left there; we hadn't eaten much at all on Friday due to the hunger suppressant quality of LSD and fish and chips before going to the pub the night before didn't count. Saturday night was to be the first real decent meal I'd had since before I had been sent down.

A wonderful meal it was too!

From the Soo-Sol it was back to the Prince of Tek where we met up with Neil, Cecil and another face I hadn't seen for a while, a fellow bass player Mick Zease. He was Mr super cool with his long black hair that flowed halfway down his back. I used to dream of having hair like his but as mine is very curly it gets as far as my shoulders and will not go any further. Mick would always talk in riddles as if he was imparting words of wisdom. He was talking a load of old bollocks most of the time really but at the time we all thought he was some kind of Guru.

There was me eighteen, going on nineteen and Mick was an ancient twenty-two so I suppose I looked upon him as being a bit more worldly wise. He had a wonderful white Fender Precision bass that he would let me borrow from time to time when I went for auditions. Eventually I would have one of my own, as well as a Fender Jazz; I wish I still had them.

Moira and I had promised ourselves that we wouldn't drink too much that evening, nor would we smoke any dope. We needed to get some rest and be bright eyed and bushy tailed for the endurance that would be the visit to my parents the next day. We were pretty good, being fairly sober when we left the pub, we smoked nothing other than normal cigarettes either.

Of course I wanted to see ma and pa but I was not looking forward to the confrontation.

++++++++++++++

Romford is way over the other side of London to Earls Court and not on the tube line. However, Newbury Park station is on the central line and a fairly short drive from Collier Row, so dad was happy to drive there to pick us up. It was still a long train ride, on the district line, from Earls Court to Mile End where we changed onto the central line to Newbury Park, in total well over an hour.

Dad was there alone, mum slaving away in the kitchen, it would be great to taste her cooking again, I still miss it to this day, especially her home made steak and kidney pie, the best I've ever tasted. In the short journey to their house dad was in good humour, chit chatting about his job, mum's job, the house yaddi, yaddi, yaddi, everything but the wedding, a blessing.

Mum was over the moon to see me and started to cry, which made me a bit tearful as well. She was a little bit flustered as she ushered us inside the house.

'It's such a lovely day,' she said, why don't you sit out in the garden; dinner will be a while yet?'

'And I bet you need a drink?' Dad asked as he raised his eyebrows whilst looking my direction.

'You bet!' I answered

'How about some sangria, before dinner?'

'Sounds wonderful!'

Dad made the best sangria ever, a bottle of red wine, a bottle of sparkling white wine, a quarter bottle of vodka, a quarter bottle of brandy, a quarter bottle of Grand Marnier with chopped lemons and oranges.

Yes it was as lethal as it sounds; I was seriously drunk before I sat down to dinner, which seemed to be swimming around my plate as I attempted to eat it. Mum had cooked my favourite, roast pork, it was a shame I was so drunk, a bit too drunk to appreciate it fully.

I think I was forgiven.

The atmosphere was not as tense as I had expected it to be; in fact both of my parents were positively friendly, if not a bit over friendly. I wasn't going to rock the boat, not today; I was enjoying my freedom too much and had no intention of changing the mood. Maybe they felt the same, having me home must have been a boost for them as well.

As we sat in the sun on that long gone Sunday afternoon it almost seemed as if the previous six months had never happened. Mum and dad were smiling and for a few hours I didn't think about Gaynes Hall or having to go back there, it was good. Moira seemed to be getting on all right with ma and pa and I wondered if maybe they were coming around to our plans.

I stood up announcing that I needed to go for a pee, on my way back from the bathroom I slipped into the kitchen to be alone with mum for a while. Maybe it was because the sangria had rushed to my head that I was feeling brave enough to talk to her about the wedding on my own.

'How's dinner coming along?' I asked

'Not so long, the meat's done, waiting for the potatoes to crisp up and just about to put the veggies on, would you like a piece of crackling?'

'Would I?' She cut me off a generous piece, I've never been able to make the crackling crisp up as well as my mother did, there is always something about home cooking, no one ever cooks the way your mother does. 'Mum, thanks for not talking about the wedding plans today.'

'Your father and I didn't want to spoil the day; we don't know when you'll be back again do we?'

'It wont be long, I'm sure I'll get the brown tie at the next tie board.'

'Oh I do hope so.' I could see a tear coming from the corner of her eye so went over to put my arms around her which made her start to cry.

'Hey, hey come on it's supposed to be a happy day today.'

'I know I just can't help feeling sad that you have to go back again.'

'You do! How do you think I feel? I can't wait to get back to those cows.' That made her laugh, 'I mean they'll be missing me, I bet the milk yield is down without me playing rock and roll to them at five in the morning.'

We pulled apart but she held my shoulders at arms length and looked at me through water filled eyes. She was smiling but there was sadness in them.

'It's not that I don't like Moira, she seems a nice enough girl, it's just that you are so young and........'

'I know mum, I know but I really want this and we do love each other.'

'Yes, I know you do; your father says I must let you make your own mistakes.'

'It's not a mis....'

'I know you don't think it is and I really, really hope that it isn't, you have our support no matter what you decide or what ever happens. You must know that we love you and only want the best for you?'

'Yes of course I do.'

'Then let's say no more about it today, go and tell your father that dinner is almost ready and to come in and sort out the wine.'

'Thanks mum.'

Those were the days of Mateus, a sparkling rose wine, it was the must have drink for Sunday dinner; dad was a beer man really and never had much taste when it came to wine. I used to quite enjoy rose at the time but I'm more of a Merlot or Shiraz man these days.

After dinner I fell asleep in the armchair, overdose of sangria and rose I think. There was an afternoon film on the TV, as usual and I hadn't seen TV for months but all I could do was fall asleep. This wasn't a real problem for me but I think everyone else was a bit miffed that I wasn't talking with them. Probably not a bad thing really, I know I'd cleared the air with mum but I'm sure it would have come up again before the end of the day.

Moira and I needed to leave at about 9pm to be able to get back to Earls Court before the last train. Mum asked us to stay over night and go back in the morning but I had an appointment with my probation officer at 10am. I didn't really want to stay over anyway, the mood up until then had been fairly light and I really wanted it to stay that way.

I didn't sleep that long but I felt somewhat groggy when I woke up. Dad was making Irish coffees; this was coffee with whiskey in it, preferably Irish whiskey, with cream floating on the top. Despite the fact that I had already consumed a considerable quantity of alcohol I said 'yes please!' Mum made sandwiches and by the time it came to leave I felt as if I could never eat again, not used to so much good food.

The journey back to Earls Court was long and uneventful; Moira and I were too tired to talk, it had been a nice day without any cross words for which I was extremely grateful. Back at Longridge Road we went straight to bed and I don't think my head hit the pillow before I was sound asleep.

+++++++++++++++++

The Borstal experience, sadly, did not stop when you were finally released, oh no Sir! Each and every one of us had to endure another two years visiting a probation officer. On Monday 19th July I had to be in the office of mine at 10am sharp. Unfortunately, sharp is not how I was feeling as I was nursing, not the world's worst hangover but a fairly close second. Not so much of a headache but I was feeling decidedly washed out. I could really have done with a couple more hours in bed instead of trying to make some idiot probation officer like me.

His office was in the Fulham Palace Road, but he turned out to be her. The man who had come to see me at Gaynes Hall had thankfully moved on. He had almost ruined my home leave when he wanted to veto my going to stay with Moira. This

Lady thankfully turned out to be somewhat different. Despite her cast iron appearance she seemed to have quite a soft nature. I can't remember her name so will refer to her as Mrs Davey, seems like as good a name as any. I would see Mrs Davey for the best part of a year from my release until Moira and I moved to Catford in 1972. However it was still July 1971 and I hadn't obtained my final release so here I was in the Fulham Palace Road.

'So, Kristopher Gray,' she looked up from my file and smiled 'I've been looking at your record and you don't exactly come over to me as a career criminal so how did you find yourself in this pickle?'

'I'm not really quite sure to be honest with you, I thought I was fire proof but it would seem that I'm not really very good at a life of crime so think I should make a career move.' Mrs Davy laughed at that; I think if was that moment when I knew that she and I were going to get on very well.

At that moment in time I was still talking about a life in farming so I was able to talk passionately to her about it. We talked for about half an hour about my plans to go to farming college, my music, Moira and the ongoing problems re the wedding plans and my parents. She seemed to understand both sides of the problem and said she would happily speak to them about it. It wasn't something I really wanted to involve her in at that point so politely declined.

'From what I can make out from the notes written by some of the officers at Gaynes Hall, you were keen to follow a career in music at one time, why the change of heart?' That was an awkward question, I'd developed the farming career to please the powers that be of Gaynes Hall but here was someone outside of my comfort zone asking me about it, I hadn't expected to have to explain myself and I hesitated. 'You don't really want to give up the music do you?'

'To be honest with you, no I don't.'

'Then why are you?'

'Again, I don't really know.'

'Maybe it's because you think that is what they want to hear at Gaynes Hall?'

Sussed! What could I say?

'Maybe,'

'Maybe? look Kristopher,'

'Please, call me Kris, only my father calls me Kristopher and usually only when he is imparting words of wisdom or telling me off.'

'OK, Kris, I'm not here to see you spend more time at Gaynes Hall than you need to so I'm not trying to catch you out. I need to assess whether you are going on the straight and narrow or back to a life of crime.'

'I do not want to go back to a life of crime; one jail term is more than enough for me!'

'Do you know something Kris? I think I believe you.' She smiled again 'I've seen a lot of Borstal boys come through these doors and I think I can tell who is straight up and who is trying to pull the wool over my eyes. I think if you hadn't been straight you would have had an answer ready for me for why you wanted to be a farmer instead of a musician.

However, I'm not sure it's the right thing for you to do, not an easy profession to be in, a bit like actors, often out of work. Still, I will be here to guide and keep a watchful eye on you.' She went back to the file for a few moments 'so tell me about the wedding, are you still planning to get married?'

'Er, yes I, er I mean yes we are but, what will you tell them at Gaynes Hall about the music and the farming?'

'What would you like me to say to them?'

'Nothing?'

'OK nothing it is, just don't let me down.'

'Trust me, easy to say I know, but I have no intention of going back inside for any reason at all.'

'OK, I trust you. So did your fiancé, Moira isn't it, come with you today?'

'Yes, she's waiting outside.'

'All right, wheel her in; I think it's time we met.'

Moira was in the waiting room reading 'Lord of the Rings' when I came out to get her.

'She wants to see me?'

'Yes she wants to see you, I think I've won her over but I think it's down to you to clinch the deal.' I could see that she was reluctant but a smile from me and she got up to follow me back to the office, but just as I was about to sit back down in the chair...

'No, no Kris, I would like to speak to Moira alone,' I looked at Moira then to Mrs Davey then back to Moira again, who looked scared shitless. Once again I smiled, but I think not as convincingly as I had before and hesitated to leave the room. 'Don't worry, she'll be quite safe with me, I won't bite.'

So, reluctantly I left the room. They weren't alone for so very long and Moira came out smiling accompanied by Mrs Davy.

'All right Kris, I think Moira and I have an understanding and I will be happy to see her next time you come to see me.'

We said our goodbyes until I eventually returned to see her later in the year.

++++++++++++++++

Monday was to be my last night of freedom before catching the train back to St Neots for an indefinite period of time. More than half the day was now gone, taken up by the fruitful visit to the probation service. Moira had gotten on with Mrs Davey like a house on fire, a lot of which she wouldn't tell and giggled at the thought of. So I felt fairly safe about what her report, which would go back to my jailers at Gaynes Hall, was going to be like. Well, there was always that nagging doubt in the back of my mind that she would grass me up re the farming and the music.

I'd been lucky with the weather, it was back when July and British summers could be relied on to be hot and sunny. Well, isn't that how we all remember the summers of our youth, only remembering the nice days? That Monday afternoon was no exception so we took the tube from Fulham Broadway to Hyde Park Corner where we spent a few hours basking in the sun and dipping our toes in the Serpentine.

We had agreed to meet some of the gang in the Prince of Tek that evening to have a farewell beer before my return on Tuesday. I can't remember everyone who was there but I can be sure of one, my good mate Neil was always up for a beer or two and that night would be no exception. As Beryl lived next door it wouldn't take much to entice her out for the evening.

A splendid night was probably had by all, too long ago and too many beers since to remember much about it.

+++++++++++++++

I don't know if it was the tension of it being my last day or the fact that I would have to return that evening, maybe both, but on Tuesday Moira and I had a serious confrontation. We had only made love on the day I came home; to be honest I'd been too stoned, drunk or exhausted to manage it since. So I thought a little bit of nookey before getting up in the morning was a good idea, I couldn't have been more wrong.

'Oh so now you want me?' She snapped 'I suppose it's because you're going back today and don't know when you'll get it again!' She grabbed the sheets to cover herself whilst pulling away from me to the far side of the bed and up against the wall.

'No! Don't be so daft.' Despite my protestations I think there was a bit of truth in what she said. 'The past few days have been a bit of a whirlwind for me and it hasn't been easy re-adjusting to being out and now I have to re-adjust to being back inside.' I reached out to touch her but she just knocked my hand away.

'I just feel as if you've moved away from me.' She scrambled out of bed, pulled a T shirt on to cover herself and went to the sink to put the kettle on, there was an awkward silence for what was probably only a minute but seemed like a lot more. 'Have you stopped loving me?' She asked whilst keeping her back to me after filing the kettle.

'NO!' I screamed back, 'of course I haven't.'

'Hmpf! Well it fucking feels like it!'

'Come on, you're being unreasonable!'

'Unreasonable? Is it unreasonable to expect the man who is supposed to love me and wants to marry me to make love to me more than once in the five days he's been home? Especially when he's been locked away for almost six months, I expected you to be rampant!'

With that she slammed the kettle down on the cooker, lit the gas and stomped out of the room slamming the door behind her. I flopped back on the bed to stare at the ceiling for some inspiration, something to tell me what to do next.

Nada!

Then suddenly, inspiration, one of our favourite albums before I was sent down had been John Lennon's first solo album, it was hardly ever off the turntable, remember them? It featured some of his most poignant and personal songs, 'Working Class Hero', 'Mother' and one of our favourite tracks 'Love', 'Love is real, Real is Love' were how the lyrics went. So I leapt naked from the bed and put it on full blast just in time for her to come back through the door. We looked at each other, she shrugged her shoulders, was there a trace of a smile? Yes there was and in no time at all we were back in the sack and making up for lost time, not once, not twice but a mind blowing three times.

We lay totally spent in bed that morning, not saying much, just alone with our thoughts. I can't say what she was thinking about, although I could hazard a guess. I had mixed thoughts, mainly centred on the impending return to captivity, but also what would I do once I achieved that final release. I had been building up my front of going to agricultural college and was beginning to wonder if it wasn't such a bad idea after all. But, and it was a big but, could I get the music out of my system, once it gets in your blood it's very difficult to get it out again.

The train was due to leave Kings Cross at around 6pm and I would be back in the dorm just in time for supper. It had been known for some to not come back from home leave, some had missed the train and arrived back late. Neither of those scenarios were going to happen to me, there was no way I was going to skip town or miss the train. There was, however, a few hours before I would have to don the suit again and make that journey. I thought if we left Earls Court around 4pm it would give us time to get to Kings Cross for some coffee and maybe something to eat. Now out of bed at midday we still had some time to ourselves.

The sun was still shining, we had something to smoke so we bought a bottle of wine and walked up to Kensington Park for an hour or so to smoke the dope and drink the wine. By 2pm it was gone and I was feeling a little bit more than mellow. We had talked and talked and talked some more, about what we would do when I came home at last, how we were going to change the world.

All total rubbish of course, we never did any of it, let alone change the world.

The time had come, the walrus said, to talk of many things, we had and we were all talked out now. So there was nothing left to do but to go back to Longridge Road and put the suit on ready for the off. We'd just been marking time all day really, some of it had been fun and some of it, for me at least, had been stressful. None of it however, had been as stressful as putting that suit back on. I knew it was going to be tough but I had no idea how tough it was going to be on both of us; it was almost like being sentenced again.

The dope and the wine were still having a marked effect on me as I changed ready for the off. We hardly spoke to each other, I think if we had said anything about my going back we would have both burst into tears, I know it was close.

Knowing that this would be a stressful moment I had asked my good friend Neil to come with us so that Moira would not have to return home alone. He was late, of course, but not too late and we made our way to the tube at Earls Court to arrive in good time at Kings Cross. Neil slipped something into my pocket when Moira went to the bathroom at the station.

'Just a little something to take the edge off things on your way back.' He smiled as he spoke to me.

'Look out for her Neil.'

'Don't worry mate, I will.' Sad to say Neil could barely look after himself let alone look after Moira, who was more than capable of looking after herself. I don't know why I asked him really, I think I wanted to make him feel that he was doing something for me, which I suppose he was.

Eventually the time came for me to board the train, I said my goodbyes to Neil and he stepped away to allow Moira and I to say our goodbyes in some privacy. We kissed and held each other for what seemed like a long time but wasn't really. Then I broke away and made my way through the barrier and onto the train. I looked back once more, I will keep the image in my mind forever of her crying uncontrollably and being led away by Neil with a comforting arm around her.

So I boarded the train.

I looked at what Neil had put in my pocket, two Mandrax tablets, Mandy's, ha, ha Mandy's make you randy, as they used to say, fat lot of good that would be for me today! Never mind, I swallowed it anyway, I'd be somewhat stoned when the train arrived in Huntingdon, great!

The other guys were all on the train, no absconders this time. We all had a few cans of beer to sup on the way. It was frowned on to arrive back drunk but no one ever got into any trouble for it, it was kind of expected, so I didn't want to let them down. Together with the Mandy and the beer I was more than just a little bit legless when I almost fell off the train at the station. Can't remember who picked us up with the bus but in no time we were back in the library. Here we changed out of our suits back into our prison blues, both physical and metaphysical. After which I stumbled back to J1 where someone kindly helped me into bed.

The cows awaited my return in the morning.

* * * * *

Chapter Six

'The Light at the End of the Tunnel'

I was back in Gaynes Hall and not feeling particularly great about it. Aside from the fact that I was nursing a phenomenal hang over from the vast amount of drugs and alcohol I had consumed before returning, I was deeply depressed. Here I was back in Borstal, voluntarily, with no idea when I might be out of here for good. I hadn't been allowed a sleep in the morning after my return and when the night watchman woke me up at the usual crack of sparrow I felt like shit. Thankfully Todd and Sid were on hand to do the bulk of the work whilst I nursed my hangover. The next tie board was exactly a week away and I was praying that I would get the discharge date this time, Bob Lewis willing of course.

A few days after my return new ties were issued, the old flat, almost kipper ties, were done away with. In came the new slimmer knitted ties, definitely a lot sexier than the old ones and I was happy to exchange my tatty old green one for the suave new design.

I hoped that I wouldn't be wearing it for too long.

I had only been back at Her Majesties pleasure a few days when the promised Young Farmers Club excursion to the Peterborough Show arrived. It was Saturday 25th July, my parents 24th wedding anniversary. All of us from the dairy, the pig house, the fattening house and the lads in the mill and the swill house were to go. No sooner had I taken off my best bib and tucker here I was putting it back on again.

We left after milking and breakfast in the mini-bus with Paddy, Gibbons and Stan, the later driving. Peterborough was less than an hour's drive away up the A1, not quite the autobahn it is today but there was certainly less traffic on it. It wasn't such a treat for me to get out of Gaynes Hall as it was for the others, I'd only just returned from home leave remember.

So as we trundled up the A1 excited at being away for a day, I started a singsong, not pop songs but the sort of thing we used to sing in the boy scouts. 'Ging, Gang Gooley', 'We're Riding Along on the Crest of a Wave', 'You'll Never Get to Heaven' and stuff like that. Childish I know but everyone was feeling up and it helped to while away the journey somewhat.

We arrived mid morning and we parked so far away it seemed to me to be in the next county as it took forever for us to walk to the show site. There were plenty of leaflets with the day's timetable, which included a motorbike display and an air sea rescue display by the Royal Navy with helicopters. Gibbons said that we could basically do and go where we wanted, he trusted us not to try and abscond. We'd all been in for a while so I thought it most unlikely that anyone would. If anyone had tried it would have put a stop to any excursion of any kind from Gaynes Hall and, if whoever did try was caught and brought back, his life would not have been worth living. It was arranged that we would meet at the bar/barbeque stall once an hour, just to be sure. That was easy for me because, as a dorm leader, I had a watch so all the dairy lads stuck with me. The others just had to keep asking people what the time was.

In no time I found a mobile Post Office, strange thing to have on the show site. They were selling prepaid letters that you could write on, stick the edges down and because it had a stamp printed on the front you could post it there and then. We were not allowed to send any mail that didn't go through the office for censoring. Here was my opportunity to send a 'bent letter', these were often sent out by lads going on home leave and would post when got home. A bit risky, not everyone was searched before they left but if you were caught with a letter for someone you would lose not just your home leave but your tie as well. It was even possible to the demoted back to the blue tie, so not many people would do it.

First class post was only three pence back then and I think the letter cost just ten in total with the postage. So I bought one, I don't really know why, I'd only been with Moira less than a week before so didn't really have much to say. I suppose it was the fact that the opportunity was there and I didn't want to miss out on the chance to send it. I told her where I was and what I was doing, although she knew about the impending trip when I had been at home. I stressed, more than once, that this was an illegal letter and she should never refer to it in any letters she wrote to me. I didn't really need to labour the point as Moira wasn't daft and understood what it was all about.

It was a really hot sunny day as I remember, and the suit was more than a little bit much for a day like that. Naturally all the ties came off and we managed to carry our jackets either over our shoulders by the hook, or tucked under the arm.

After the first hour had gone by we all met up with Gibbons to check in. There were a number of businesses selling farm related stuff from Wellington boots to tractors and combine harvesters. In amongst all of the farm gear was a Vox Amplification stand, Todd and I found a music stand, Wow, what an absolute dream come true! Vox still made guitars in those days so Todd and I gingerly made our way to the stand were they had amps, guitars and a drum kit. There were a few people milling about, strumming a few chords, twiddling with amps and generally being interested in what they had to offer.

'Can I help you lads?' someone, with a Vox identity tag on his jacket asked us, 'would you like to come up and have a closer look? Do you play at all?'

'Yes I play guitar,' I told him, 'and my mate here plays a mean harp.'

'Well, I'm sorry but we don't have any harps.'

'I've got my own,' he said as he cocked his head towards him whilst quickly whipping out his harp from his inside pocket and waving it before Mr Vox's eyes.

'OK guys, I play drums, my colleague here plays the bass, would you like to come up and jam with us?'

'Would we?' I replied 'Just try and stop us!'

They had a beautiful pearl drop guitar, the kind that Brian Jones of the Rolling Stones used to have; I wish I had one of them now. I can't remember what bass his mate was playing but it was probably something nice and highly sort after these days. So for almost the next hour we jammed, mostly twelve bar blues, it was escapism of the best kind.

Sadly we eventually had to go; it was time to rendezvous with Gibbons. We said our goodbyes to the Vox crowd, as we had drawn a bit of an audience, and told the guys on the stand we had to meet our friends for lunch, which was basically true. We'd brought packed lunches and as a special treat Gibbons and Paddy bought us all a pint each from the bar. It was a welcome treat indeed. After which we made our way, altogether, to watch the motorbike display.

It was a very impressive display, which included jumping alternately through hoops of fire. I've never had a thing about motorbikes since I was taken on a hair-raising trip from Romford to Southend at the speed of sound whilst hanging onto my mate for dear life. You didn't have to wear crash helmets in those days and I wasn't as we hurtled down the A13 late at night, very scary! Needless to say I gushed and awed in all the right places, it was after all a very professional display. There was just no way I would ever consider doing such a thing.

Once that display was over we went back to the bar for another beer, this time paid for by Paddy who told us it was a reward for being great workers on the farm. It was a shame Phil had already gone, it would have been fun if he'd been there as well, better for him though. After two pints on a hot sunny day, I was feeling a little light headed. Despite having had a considerable amount to drink on my home leave, I still wasn't really used to drinking again. However there was a very convivial atmosphere between prison staff and inmates on this sunny carefree day.

Lunchtime was soon over and the Royal Navy Rescue display was due to start. I was actually quite keen to see it as my father had been in the RN during the war. I can remember as a young boy having ambitions to join up when I left school. My father always did his best to dissuade me from doing so. He needn't have worried as by the time I was eleven I had discovered The Beatles and guitars and the Navy was history. Maybe if I had pursued that particular career route I would not have found myself in the predicament I now did. Still now is not the time to dwell on if's, buts and maybe's I was having a fun day anyway.

Needless to say the RN put on an absolutely stunning display which; if I hadn't been committed to another career path, might have persuaded me to join up there and then. There were helicopters and rubber dinghies as they simulated people being rescued at sea. They had my confidence; if ever I needed someone to rescue me these were the boys.

One stand that made us all laugh, including Paddy and Gibbons, was the recruitment stand for Her Majesties Prison Service. Can you believe that? In the middle of the East of England show, with a busload of Borstal boys running loose, there was a recruiting centre for screws. Of course we had to go and make ourselves known and I could see it made them a little uncomfortable.

What a laugh that was.

The day seemed to be over in no time as the sun, although still a long way from going down as the longest day had only just passed, was still way past the yardarm. Wearily we trudged our way back to the mini bus, which was even further out there in the prairie than I had originally thought. I felt sorry for Stan, who had to drive us back, if he was anywhere near as tired as we were I don't know how he did it.

It was good that the dairy boys could catch a little bit of shut eye during the journey back as we had to go back to work on our return. Those cows don't milk themselves you know and they were pretty desperate by the time we got them into the milking shed. By the end of the milking session my brain was totally fried and I was in bed as soon as supper had finished.

All in all it had been a great day out, which, forty years later, I still have vivid memories of, especially the jam session on the Vox stand.

I wish I had one of those Vox Pearl Drop guitars now, worth a bloody fortune.

+++++++++++++++++

Eventually the week ground its way forward and the 29th of July, tie board day, arrived. There were a number of expectations that day other than myself; Russell amongst them, also hoping to receive his discharge. There was also expectations of red and green ties, Jock was up for his green tie on a three month but I doubted that he would get it, I was right.

My time had come and I was wheeled into the office to face Hawkes, Lewis and the representative of the board of visitors.

'Hello Gray,' Hawks smiled at me, I'd learnt not to read anything into smiles. 'I'm pleased to say that we are awarding you your discharge; you have first date which is the first of September. I have to say you have been a model inmate and I personally will be sorry to see you go. I, along with the majority of officers here do not believe you will ever return here or to any other penal establishment. I think you have learnt a lesson here and I feel confident you will become a model citizen, congratulations.'

I came out of the office with my head swimming, I quickly realised that I would only be spending two weeks more there than if I had received my discharge at the last tie board. Had I been awarded a one month on my green tie I would have had the second date discharge. I was elated, of course and I knew that Moira and my parents would be calling that evening to find out the results of the tie board. I was excited to know how they would react, wishing that I could see their faces as they received the news.

Sadly Russell, my deputy dorm leader and friend, did not receive his discharge date, I would have come and gone but Russell would still be there.

In a mere four weeks I would be leaving J1 and going to the discharge unit where I would spend my two last weeks in Gaynes Hall.

During those last four weeks one of the main topics of conversation, both privately and during dorm agro, was the OZ trial.

For those of you who do not remember or even, were not born at the time, it was a famous obscenity trial. During the late sixties and early seventies there were a number of so called 'underground newspapers', the alternative press. Amongst them were, Friendz The International Times, better know as IT and the aforementioned OZ. These magazines were, mostly, fuelled and written by dope smoking, acid dropping hippies of the time. I read them avidly. OZ was started by Richard Neville and Jim Anderson in Australia in the early sixties, hence the name and brought to the UK in 1966 where they recruited one Felix Dennis, who was selling early copies on the street.

During the early part of 1971 they produced what became known as 'The Schoolboy Issue', this was their downfall. This name was widely misunderstood to mean that it was intended for school children. Whereas the meaning had been that is was created by schoolboys after the editors invited a number of secondary students, including the young Charles Shaar Murray, to edit a copy of the magazine.

The Establishment hated the underground press and the Schoolboy Issue featured a sexualised parody of Rupert the Bear created by a 15 year old schoolboy by pasting the head of Rupert onto the lead character from an X rated cartoon, which was deemed obscene. It wasn't the actual articles that the law prosecuted them for but for the fact that some of them were sent via the Royal Mail. Back in those days it was illegal to send pornographic material through the post, it probably still is but who cares? Had they just been charged with obscenity they would have faced a maximum fine of £100 but, they were charged with conspiracy to corrupt public morals, an archaic charge that carried an unlimited penalty.

The celebrated barrister, John Mortimer, a famous playwright, author and creator of 'Rumpole of the Bailey' stood for the defence of Dennis and Anderson while Neville represented himself. A considerable number of well-known faces, including the famous groupie Caroline Coon, jazz musician George Melly and former pirate DJ John Peel were wheeled in to give evidence in their defence. John Lennon and Yoko Ono joined a protest march against the prosecution and recorded a single under the name 'The Elastic Oz Band' called 'God Save Us All'. But, to no avail, the Establishment wanted their heads and after a lengthy and expensive trial they were found guilty and sentenced to up to fifteen months in jail. The papers were either full of how these hippies would be taken down a peg or two or what an injustice the whole thing was.

Needless to say all of us Borstal boys were on the side of the poor editors of OZ; we saw this as taking a hammer to crack a nut. Even the officer who took dorm agro that week, and I can't for the life of me remember who that was, agreed it was futile.

In a matter of days they were all released on bail, pending an appeal. The newspapers featured photographs of the three editors with their previously long locks shorn. Even if they were not robbed of their freedom they would have been robbed of their dignity, I could empathise with that.

The outcry over the trial sparked a major corruption inquiry which ended in the jailing of the senior office responsible for the prosecution. Also, around 400 officers were either jailed or left the force due to the corruption investigations that followed. It was deemed that far worse pornographic material could be bought over the counter in Soho than was featured in that issue of OZ.

The case, held at the infamous Old Bailey, was the longest obscenity trial in British legal history and was a tremendous talking point for us Borstal boys.

++++++++++++++

Oliver, one of the J1, whom I become friends with, had been released a few weeks before the tie board and he wrote to me just after it. He asked if I had managed to get my discharge and also asked after Russell, I wrote back to him to give the good and bad news, I had intended to keep in touch but of course, never did. I recently found the letter I had from him, almost forty years ago; I wonder where he is now?

The entertainments committee had one last gig to do before I left; the local Vicar's tea party, which was a Sunday afternoon affair. We still had the same team that had been together since its inception when I had first arrived. The only change had been Kevin being discharged and Todd taking his place, there was definitely a dearth of talent in Gaynes Hall whilst I was there.

It wasn't a particularly memorable afternoon, unlike the cricket club, it was mostly elderly ladies in twin sets and pearls sipping tea and eating cucumber sandwiches. I don't think my Beatles and hippie songs went down that well, nor the blues jams Todd and I performed. Quite frankly I didn't give a shit, I now had a discharge date and I was going home, tea party or no tea party.

Ok it was nice to get away for an afternoon but I would have been just as happy to be sitting up on the farm with the cows. The ladies were polite enough and the Vicar did his level best to make us feel welcome, but for me, the magic had gone. It had been fun before; when the light at the end of the tunnel had been so feint I could barely see it. However, now it was shining brightly and I wanted to get to it so much I couldn't get excited about anything else.

I don't think anyone really noticed that I wasn't on form but I certainly didn't feel as if I was. However, there were many thanks from everyone there.

Perhaps it was just me.

+++++++++++++++

It felt like I was now just marking time before going into the discharge unit. Saturday morning inspections were a pain in the arse that I couldn't get out of. I even found visits from Moira and my parents a chore as well. Now that I had a discharge date Moira had confirmed the wedding date as the 9th of

October. There would be a reception in a hotel in Kensington High Street and we would be going on honeymoon in Paris. Can you imagine that, from Borstal to Paris in less than a month? I was looking forward to it all, really I was but I just can't explain how I felt during those last few weeks before the discharge unit.

Mrs Davey my new and somewhat more agreeable probation officer came to visit me at the beginning of August to make sure everything was all right. I was pleased she had taken over my case rather than the miserable bugger who almost screwed up my home leave. I knew that I would get on with her on my release; after all I had to go and see her once a month. We had a pleasant half hour or so visit during which she congratulated me on my up coming nuptials, hoping that we would be very happy. The idea of having to check in every month wasn't that exciting but at least I didn't think it would be that bad after all.

Just as I was thinking that everything was going along swimmingly a bombshell hit me, right between the eyes. We'd had two new arrivals in J1, Steve Evans and Peter Hunt; they'd only been there a couple of weeks when one night they decided to go over the wall together. I was furious; I really felt that it reflected on me and my leadership of the dorm.

Hawks was very sympathetic.

'Has there been any trouble with them in the dorm, anyone giving them a hard time?' he asked me.

'No!' I replied emphatically

'Well don't worry you won't be held to blame.' That was something I felt pleased about. The two of them were captured the next day hiding in a barn somewhere not that far away. They were brought back to spend a week in the block and surprisingly returned to the dorm. Nobody had appreciated their absconding as it reflected badly on, not just me, but all of us.

I know I have mentioned absconders before but I should mention one of the more famous and amusing cases in the history of Gaynes Hall. Although this didn't take place during my tenure I feel it is worth mentioning here. The alternative comic Malcolm Hardee had also fallen foul of the law in 1970 and been sent to Gaynes Hall. Unlike me he had made friends with the resident vicar who took him, and a number of others, for a few days to a place called 'The retreat'. This was a monastery, I don't know where, but he said, although the food was better it drove him mad because it was a silent order.

So one night he donned a habit with only his underwear as well, and made good his escape. He decided to head north to a pen pals house in Leeds because he figured that they would think he had gone south, being from south London. He was given a lift by a vicar's wife who was suspicious of his boots and subsequently called the police. They were eventually waiting for him at the pen pals house and he was shipped back to the Scrubs and re allocated to Dover Borstal, a closed and very hard place indeed. He was eventually released during the same week that I was sentenced and went on to have a career on the comedy circuit but sadly died in 2006 in a boating accident.

+++++++++++++++

I was due to go into the discharge unit two weeks before my discharge date. However, before I could do that I had to first see the board of visitors and also be interviewed by all three housemasters to see if I was a suitable candidate for the unit. How could I not be? I mean I had been deemed suitable for release so how could I not be suitable for the discharge unit. I think this was just another hoop they wanted us to jump through to keep us on our toes.

The discharge unit was a world of its own; there were no roll calls or supervision of any kind. There was no curfew as such, we could go to bed when we wanted, however; we still had to get up at the same time. There was no night watchman either so I would have to get myself up for the early morning milking session; there were alarm clocks for that. All meals would be eaten in the unit after being ordered from a menu and we had our own tea and coffee making facilities. It would be a blessed relief from life as it had been in the dormitories.

And, there was a television.

However, I would first have to get past the Spanish Inquisition that was the unit interview and the board of visitors. Needless to say it was a doddle; the board of visitors were more than pleased with how I had behaved during my stay. They were convinced that I was a reformed character and would be a model citizen in the future. They said they would be interested to known what college I would eventually go to and would keep in close contact with my probation officer. I didn't like to tell them that going to farming college was the last thing on my mind but I felt it wasn't the right time to do so.

Next up was the interview for the discharge unit, there was Ron Hawks and the other two housemasters sitting before me like the three wise monkeys. Hawks was in the middle, I suppose because he was my house master, and flanked by the other two house masters. They asked a number of inane questions about what I thought it meant by going to the unit and if I thought I could act responsibly.

I mean, what did they expect me to say? I'm looking forward to spending half the night awake and rampaging through the camp at three in the morning. I don't think anyone was ever refused entry to the discharge unit, well not during the time I was there anyway.

In the meantime there were still a few Saturday morning inspections to go through, which we did without too much strain.

I think we won the shield a couple of times more before I moved out to the unit but we never came last, as the worst dorm of the week.

There was the question of my successor however, when I went to the discharge unit there would need to be a new dorm leader for J1. The normal course of events would mean, if he wasn't being discharged as well, the deputy would take over and a new one put in his place. Sadly, the powers that be didn't consider Russell to be dorm leader material, I could do no more than agree with them. I actually thought that Jock would have been a good choice and I told them so.

Unfortunately I was outvoted and they decided to draft in Frank Dwyer from J3. This was not a popular decision amongst the inmates of J1 who felt that someone from within should have been promoted. I had to agree, I thought that it would lead to problems, the lads would give him trouble and he would go over the top in making his presence felt. Thankfully I wouldn't be there to have to sort out the mess. I did have a pep talk with everyone the night before I moved out to the unit; I particularly looked towards Russell, Jock and Alan Mitchell to keep the others in line.

I know it wouldn't have reflected on me but I'd bought into the system, played it for my own ends and wanted to see it work when I was long gone. Everything seemed to work out all right, I don't think Frank was too happy about leaving his friends in J3 any more than J1 wanted to welcome him with open arms. On my few, brief visits after I went into the unit; everything seemed to be working out all right.

++++++++++++++++

Of course I was accepted into the discharge unit, along with two other lads that I had been on the reception party with, Ginger Bates and Paul Masters. Whereas I had been on a three month red and a two month green, theirs were four and one, same time only a different way, not sure what I would have preferred. I think there were a dozen of us all together.

So on the morning of the 18th of August the current inhabitants of the unit, after breakfast, donned their suits, said their farewells in the dining hall, and then boarded the mini bus that would transport them to the station and freedom. After I had finished the morning milking session I went back to J1 to gather up my kit and take it over to the unit, I was no longer a member of that dorm, nor its leader, I was on my way out.

Well, not for another two, painfully long weeks anyway.

As I lifted my kit in my bed sheet to leave the top bed space in J1, the corner by the door, I felt a little bit sad. Yes of course I was excited that I would now be in the discharge unit. I was leaving behind the last almost seven months of my life with mostly good memories, if you can have such a thing in a Borstal. Although not something I would care to repeat, it had been nowhere near as bad as I had expected it to be. The space was now reserved for the new dorm leader, Frank Dwyer, and I closed the door of J1 for, almost, the last time.

The other new unit inmates had moved in after breakfast. There were enough rooms for all of us to have one each so I had to settle for what was left, which wasn't much different to the others. It was small, with a bed and bedside cabinet but good enough for me. We had a small dining area that doubled as a TV room where we could also make our own tea a coffee.

TV, now that would be a novelty, I hadn't even seen TV on my home leave as Moira didn't have one and I only saw something briefly at my parents. When anyone came back from their home leave they would especially talk about a series called 'Budgie' which featured Adam Faith as a small time petty crook who was always getting into scrapes, a kind of light hearted look at the crime world of the early seventies. You have to remember the Kray twins had only been sent to prison a couple of years before and the corruption in the UK police forces, especially the Met in London, was still rife. Remember the OZ trial and how it was shown that the police took numerous backhanders from pornography sellers back then?

It wasn't just them.

That first lunchtime was the first time we all sat down together to have eat on our own without anyone looking over our shoulders, it was exhilarating. I knew some of the other lads and a few I didn't know at all, although I knew the faces and of course I knew Ginger and Paul who had also been in Jupiter house.

After dinner on the first night we watched TV, because we could, it was the first time that I saw UFO. This was the first live action series from Gerry Anderson, the creator of Thunderbirds, amongst others. It was set in 1990 and featured a covert unit that was fighting aliens trying to take over the earth. It only ran for one season, sadly, and looks very dated now, especially as 1990 came and went twenty years ago but I can still watch the re-runs on satellite. It featured the extremely sexy Gabrielle Drake, sister of the singer Nick Drake who had died at a very early age at the height of his success. It was worth watching if only for her.

There was no supervision of any kind in the unit, well after all who was going to try and abscond? I know someone had once been caught smoking dope in there but I think it was considered a one off. There was no curfew or any lights out time, we could stay up all night if we wanted to, as long as we were at work on time that is. So that first night I think we were up until gone two in the morning, yes even I was despite having been up since the crack of sparra'.

There was also no night-watchman coming around every hour to check on us, nor any red light in the room. For the first time in almost seven months, I slept in the dark. We had alarm clocks to wake us up as no member of staff would come to do it. I had my own because I had to be up before anyone else but the others took turns in waking the others in the morning. Those who were on the brown/discharge tie were not required to march anywhere but still had to go on parade in the morning and lunch times. Those of us in the discharge unit were not required to go on parade either. As I had not been on parade in the mornings and rarely in the afternoons because of my position on the farm, it didn't really make any difference to me. Still it was another privilege for the others.

I felt like shit the next day having had about two hours sleep, still I could do things like that in those days. So I was in bed a damn sight earlier that night. We did get into a routine, when the novelty of being able to stay up until all hours wore off, and were mostly in bed by midnight.

There was no twenty four hour television in those days which probably helped.

++++++++++++++

Moira had come to visit on the 8th of August and my parents, for the last time, the following week. Moira would come for the last time on the 22nd, sports day, which was an open day. All families were invited and it did not affect your visiting orders, Mum and dad agreed that it should be Moira's day as I would be out the following week. So Moira came up on what turned out to be, a very hot August day

There were all kinds of sporting events, that we weren't really interested in but it was good to show Moira off, in her hot pant suit, to those who still had untold to do. Because I was in the discharge unit I could go anywhere I wanted to in the camp with whomsoever I wanted to.

So........

'Would you like to come up to the farm and see where I have been working all this time?' I asked Moira

'Why not?' she replied.

So off we went with our arms around each other to go and see the farm. On the way I took a detour to the field where the herd was grazing to show them to her. My favourite, Jo, who was always happy to see me, came up to the gate to say hello. I think Moira was a little bit wary of her but in no time could see that she wasn't a threat.

From there we went to the farm which was completely deserted as it was too early for milking and every one else, staff included, were at the field for the sports events. So I showed her the fattening house, the pig pens, the mill and finally the dairy where I explained all the milking process.

'So,' I asked tentatively 'would you like me to make you a cup of tea or do you fancy a fuck?' you should have seen the look on her face, 'well?'

'Don't be daft,' she said 'we can't do that!'

'Why not?' I replied 'There's no one here but us, everyone is down at the camp drinking tea or orange squash watching the sports events. I'm up for it, how about you?'

I'm sure you've heard of a tumble in the hay, an expression used to describe having sex. Well, on that day Moira and I had a tumble in the hay, the only time I've ever done it in a haystack. Oh how we laughed, it was over in no time at all but what a quickie it was. I think the danger of doing it was part of the buzz, although I knew there was little or no chance of being caught. I'm not sure what would have happened if we had, maybe I'd have lost my discharge, was it really that big an offence?

After picking out the bits of hay from our clothes and parts of our anatomy we wandered back down to the camp. Here I had to suffer the jeers from my ex dorm mates and fellow unit inhabitants.

'What you two been up to then?'

'Couldn't wait till next week?'

'Hope you didn't make a mess up there!' and variations on the theme. I said nothing, preferring to let them believe what they wanted to believe and bask in the knowledge that I had done what they would have loved to be able to do. There were even a few members of staff who gave me a sideways look as if to say 'well did you?' I wasn't confessing to anything, maybe Moira looked a little bit more embarrassed and guilty than I did, I didn't care, I wanted them all to be jealous without me saying a word.

Eventually the day was over and Moira along with a whole bunch of mothers, fathers and girlfriends finally had to leave. It was an emotional parting for the two of us with the knowledge that the next time we saw each other would be with me as a free man.

This was only ten days away, and it couldn't come soon enough.

+++++++++++++++

Of course there was no inspection on Saturday mornings in the unit, nor did we have to get up early at the weekend, unless we wanted breakfast that is. I had to get up of course because of the milking but I didn't mind doing that, I preferred to keep on working right up till the end as it was better than twiddling my thumbs and waiting for the final day.

We did have a lot of fun in the unit; one of the most memorable events was a midnight walk to Grafton Water. I don't know how far away from the camp that was but it was a fair old stroll. I remember sitting by the lake with the rest of the lads and pondering philosophically on the last few months. It had been an experience, I'm not sure I would say I wouldn't have missed it for the world but I think if I hadn't had it things could have been a lot worse.

It was a clear night and I can see it just like it was yesterday. It was a warm evening and the moon was reflecting on the lake. I could almost imagine what it would have been like if I had been able to drop a tab of acid. It would have been the perfect trip.

There was one more tie board on the 24th of August, one week before my discharge. Of course I didn't have to go before it but I was glad to learn that Russell was finally awarded his; he'd been there for over a year, a long time for Gaynes Hall.

Eventually the 31st of August came around, the day before my discharge. It was my last day on the farm and I went round to say my goodbyes to everyone on the farm course. Gibbons and Paddy said that they would be sorry to lose me as I had been the best number one dairy boy they had ever had.

I bet they said that to all the boys.

Then, once the afternoon milking was over, I officially handed over the reigns to Todd who would now become the number one and Sid, who I had come in with, would be number two although I don't think it would have been for long. I said my goodbyes to the herd and went back to the unit for the last evening and the last supper.

The excitement of the impending morning and our release kept us all awake that night. We talked about what we would do and how we would never find ourselves inside ever again. I do remember Ginger telling us about how he had been a burglar and could break into anywhere with just a scrubbing brush and a spoon. We all laughed, of course and set him the task of proving it. So we closed all the windows in the TV room, shut them really tight and left him to work his magic, and work it he did. While we all waited outside the room Ginger went outside the unit armed with his brush and spoon. In no time he came out of the TV room having made his entry via the window.

To this day I have no idea how he did it but we all laughed till our sides ached.

+++++++++++++++

So here I am, at the same point where I started this narrative, in the library of Gaynes Hall. Wearing my suit, waiting for the mini bus to take me to the station and home to Moira. We had all barely slept the night before. It was a bit like Christmas Eve as a kid, or the night before you went on your summer holidays.

All we could do was talk about the next day.

We had breakfast in the unit then went over to the dining room to say goodbye to every one, including certain members of staff. After we changed into our suits we had to hand in all our kit, I was glad to see the back of it all.

Together with the rest of the inmates of the discharge unit I boarded the mini bus to be taken to the station. We all shook hands with the officer who drove us there, and then he left us, free men.

It had been two hundred and nineteen days and an early after I had been sentenced.

Free at last!

* * * * *

Epilogue

I was finally released on the first of September 1971 and went back to Earls Court and Moira. We were married, on the 9th October, (John Lennon's thirty first birthday,) as she had planned. The service took place at the church in Redcliffe Gardens South Kensington and we went on to Kensington High Street to the Kensington Hotel for the reception. It almost went off without a hitch, other than the hotel staff managed to drop an enormous tray of trifle, which made a considerable mess on the floor. We then had our honeymoon in Paris.

We eventually moved out of Earls Court in 1972 having bought a flat in Lewisham. Then after having a son in 1973 we parted company in 1975 when he was two, but that is all another story.

I did go back to Gaynes Hall, on the open day in 1972, almost a year after I was released. The staff hadn't changed and there was one lad who had been there when I was. He had been discharged but had re-offended whilst still on probation so they sent him back. I went, primarily, to show off my re-grown hair and beard, which made me look a bit like Edgar Broughton.

Gaynes Hall, the main house, was built in 1800 by George Byfield. During world war two it was used by the SOE, Special Operations Unit, training spies. After the war it was used as a Borstal until 1983 when the system was scrapped. The house was bought by a consulting company and renovated then sold in 1990 to the Angela Malik School of Food and Wine, who still operate there.

It is a grade 2 listed building.

The camp was demolished and a new category C prison, Littlehey, was built for adult men and opened in 1988. I had intended to go back twenty five years later, but never did.

Of all the inmates I served time with I have seen but a handful since. I once bumped into Alan Welch, around 1977 when I saw him shop lifting a bag of sugar from a corner shop in Penge. When I stopped him he thought I was the store detective. We went to his flat for a cup of tea, chewed over old times and then I never saw him again. A couple of years later I was working as a mini cab driver whilst trying to make it in the music business. One day a new driver started and it took a few days for me to twig that it was Andy from the entertainments committee. We talked about doing this book together, I don't know why we didn't, and then he was gone again.

Whilst I was still together with Moira I saw Todd at Clapham Junction station, he said he didn't remember me, perhaps he didn't want to. I also saw Russell at Ronnie Scott's club when I went to see a band, which were friends of mine; play there, also in the seventies. He remembered me all right; needless to say he wasn't with Pip and seemed very bitter about how his life had turned out since the Gaynes Hall days.

Since I started writing this book I have made contact with a number of people who were at Gaynes Hall around the time I was, who have helped to jog my memory about certain aspects of life there. This includes Alan Mitchell who I found on the friend's reunited site, we've spoken on the phone and I hope to meet up with him one day, he was one of the best at the time.

I'd like to thank my wife, Ziggy, for encouraging me to write this book in the first place and who did the best job of proof reading, despite being German, Cathy Kowan, for her tips and advice, Sheila Machray, also for proof reading and letting me use her pen to start writing it almost forty years ago. Thanks also to my old mate Terry Rawlings for reading and offering more advice and last but by no means least all the old inmates of Gaynes Hall, without whom I could not have written this book. If you recognise yourself in these pages please feel free to contact me via my website www.krisgray.co.uk it would be fab to hear from you.

Kris Gray
June 2010